ROBIN RAINBOW

HOW TO GET CUSTOMERS TO PAY

... Getting customers to pay made easy ...

ISBN: 1451550650
ISBN-13: 9781451550658

CONTENTS

ETHICS

If you buy on credit, do your best to pay on due date. If you sell on credit, never be shy to ask for payment if it's overdue. It's your money, so get it!

Failing to pay debts is not just dishonourable, it is theft. "Give to Caesar what is Caesar's, and to God what is God's." (Matt 22:21**). "Give everyone what you owe him." (**Romans 13:7**).**

NOTICE

This book is a credit control and debtor management guide only. It is not legal advice and persons using or adapting the contents do so entirely at their own risk. As any such usage is beyond the control of the author and publisher no liability can be accepted. Legal advice should be sought to meet your specific needs or those of your business.

PANIC BUTTON - GET PAID!

Do you have a crisis because customers haven't paid? If so, read Chapters 23 & 24 now and the rest straightaway after buying *Get Paid!* If it isn't that bad yet, read chapters 8, 9, 11 and 12 now and the rest as soon as possible. If things are a bit wobbly, read the Scary Credit section of Chapter 4, then buy this and start at the beginning to stop the wobble and get paid painlessly. *Get paid!* helps you get your money regardless of the size of your business and is especially helpful for small businesses.

Smaller businesses are being squeezed by big ones bent on making them pay sooner by reducing payment terms from 30 days to 14 days, or less. But some want to have their cake and eat it by paying their creditors late – especially small businesses lacking the means to prevent it.

Get Paid! gives you the means to get paid more or less on time without upsetting customers, or stressing yourself or your staff. It's your money, so get it! *Get Paid!* also helps you to avoid giving credit to those with a less than perfect reputation.

*If you were a printer and got this label job,
would you grant him credit?*

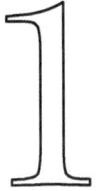

GET PAID NOW

*A sale is not a sale until
the money's in the till...*
(origin uncertain, but it's true)

Would you give a personal guarantee to a bank, or other lender, to let your business lend money free of charge to customers? Lending money for free is what you do when giving credit and if a major customer defaults (jargon for doesn't pay) and your business collapses, you could lose your shirt or skirt and much more.

Getting paid in the second decade of the 21st century will be harder than it has been for years, so never be shy to ask for your money. Keep this book on your desk and use it to get paid without stressing yourself.

Unless you are skilful, or lucky, getting paid has rarely been easy. Depending on the business climate it has ranged from troublesome to tough, especially for small businesses and professional firms. A rare easy cycle ended with the global financial crisis when it skipped the troublesome phase and turned tough as liquidity problems (jargon for no money) hit much of the world. This forced the banks to tighten-up on lending, which alone would have made getting paid harder, but it was worsened by the downturn that followed. By June 2009 one business went bankrupt every 8 minutes (source: Dun & Bradstreet; June, 2009) which meant they failed to pay their creditors, and sometimes their bank. Burnt fingers make banks cautious and as they are unlikely to quickly forget the pain, business lending criteria will remain strict and more securities required. This means it will be a long time before getting paid gets easy again.

If you are in business, especially a small business or professional practice, make getting paid a priority. For those short of time, this book gives as much practical help as some costly credit control seminars and will help you through difficult situations. At the end of most chapters is a box to write your tactics for solving payment problems if they differ from ours - you will soon know which ones work!

As well as helping to solve payment problems for those in small to mid size businesses and professional practices this book also helps people in larger outfits who have to ask for money. Over 60% of businesses sell on credit to other businesses (they have to because their rivals do and customers demand it) and at least 90% of these businesses are small to medium size, depending on the definition of *small*. Credit control in smaller outfits is harder than it is in big ones. Small firms do not employ credit controllers so the owners, or other staff, have to do the disliked task of persuading customers to pay. But hesitate before getting the sales team to do credit control by saying; *you made the sale, so you get the money* because that can reduce future sales. It can also fail to obtain prompt payment as shown in the *Selecting your credit controller* chapter. If you must get sales people to ask for money, give them each a copy of this book and inspire them with the intimate relationship between getting sales, getting payment and their income.

Making credit control fun (it's quite easy) helps you to get debtors to pay promptly without fuss. You can also get more sales at the same time because credit control, done properly, is a sales tool as well as a money-gathering exercise. If you do not like asking for money, outsourcing the task may be a solution. But whatever you decide, someone must ask for payment because if you don't get paid you go broke. When money is short, and sometimes even when it isn't, some businesses only pay when asked.

Business-to-Business (B2B) payment records show that big outfits pay their bills later than smaller ones - those with 500+ employees can take more than double the standard term before paying. They also tend to pay smaller firms last because many small businesses are not good at asking for money. B2B payment records have rarely been perfect, but that does not mean *your business* has to suffer. Even when money is plentiful, around 40% of businesses pay late, but when money is tight the majority pay late; often 50 to 90 days late (sources: Dun & Bradstreet and Experian), so look after your money and be careful who you lend it to ...

HERE ARE FIVE MONEY-LENDING SURVIVAL TIPS:

1. Work out the risk;
2. Get debtors to pay promptly;
3. Be firm without being abusive – you want them to buy from you again;

4. Have a structured reminder system;
5. Look at outsourcing your receivables – it can be cheaper and more effective than keeping it in-house.

Doing nothing about late-payers encourages them to continue abusing your interest free loan. This guide shows how to help them break the habit.

RISK

Those who hesitate lose money, so get paid because it is your money and not theirs. Even if your customer does not go broke, letting them pay late costs you money because few firms, especially small ones, charge interest on overdue accounts. You can if it is specified in your terms and conditions of trade (see *Terms & Conditions of Trade* chapter) and possibly can even if it is not. But better to be paid on time than being your customers' bank.

While payment delays can quickly worsen, they only improve slowly. Improvement starts when suppliers put the pressure on, but this takes time because they procrastinate. Procrastination increases the risk of losing money, as the more time slow payers are given, the bigger the risk of them becoming non-payers. It is also risky to go easy on 'special accounts' – for your cousin, old college friend, drinking partner and the like. A lot of money has been lost through special accounts with friends and relatives.

Bad debt risk begins immediately a customer walks out of the door with your goods or services bought on credit. Those who ask to be paid and are persistent in a business-like manner stand a much better chance of getting paid than those who do little or nothing. Just hoping that payment is in the mail, or the money is in cyberspace, increases default risk. Although taking 50 or 60 days to pay is common, it is reasonably easy to make it uncommon in your business.

The following chart shows how rapidly bad debt risk increases with time:-

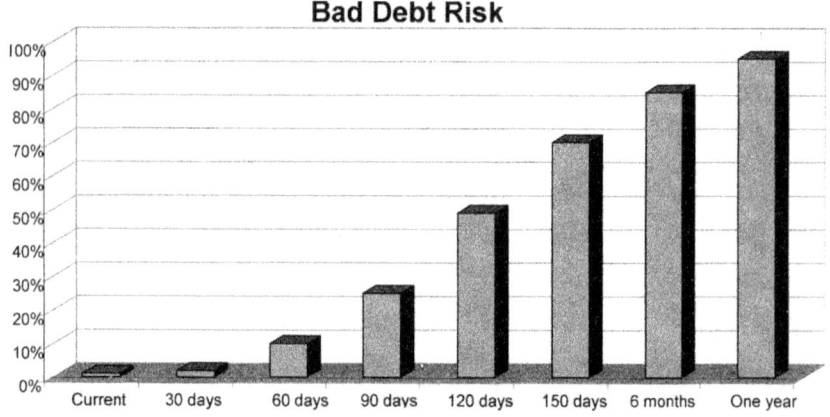

Source: Accounts Receivable Solutions Ltd data from 1998 to 2009

In the thrill of getting more business, bad debt risk can take the back seat. But an asset (your goods or services) are only an asset if they remain under your control. If you do not get paid, the asset will be lost unless you repossess it, which can be hard, so a sale is not a sale until the money is in the till. Before giving credit, ensure that the customer can and will pay by doing credit checks beforehand as shown in the next chapter. Then use this book to get paid, because when the money comes in a sale really is a sale and not a loss.

Tackle slow-payers as soon as possible, because when your money is 30 days overdue you have a 2% bad debt risk. At 60 days the risk is 8%, at 90 days it is 22% and at 120 days there is almost a one-in-two chance of never getting your money. Thereafter non-payment risk rises dramatically and after a year total loss is almost totally certain. If non-payment is due to a dispute, a compromise may be necessary. If the customer goes broke, payment to unsecured creditors by receivers and liquidators is rare and then usually only a few cents in the dollar.

The previous bad debt statistics are sourced from the author's company and are similar to those published by the Law League of America some years ago. Similar conclusions have been arrived at by banks who also regard debtors as high risk securities. Even in good times most only value them at 30% to 50% of book value – in tough times they can be reluctant to place any value on them. Most banks have lost money by incurring bad debts, some have gone spectacularly broke, others propped up by government, or owned by them, and many have been intensely criticised for sloppy lending practices. You can avoid being a sloppy lender by refusing credit to those who might not pay. If you are dying to get the business, give them a big cash discount instead of credit. If they do not accept it because they need the credit, can you afford to have them as a customer?

The how-to-get-paid methods in this book are used by the Accounts Receivable Solutions outsource credit control and debtor management team in several countries - with local variations they apply to Australia, USA, Canada, New Zealand, UK, South Africa and other English speaking countries. They can get you paid (sometimes large sums) when others methods have failed. $5,000, which was a large amount for one small business, was recovered from a shaky customer who went bust shortly afterwards and the other unsecured creditors lost all their money. If you get paid when others fail to, don't worry too much about that little nasty called *voidable preference*. *Voidable Preference* can be called different names but they are all claw-back attempts by receivers, or others who claim you have been unfairly paid. In practice, possession by you of your own money can be nine-tenths of the law provided the amount is modest. In liquidator or receiver-speak, this means that the amount recovered has to exceed the cost of recovery (their time and legal costs).

If you are ever in the situation where a receiver or someone else says, *'even if it is your money, pay it to me or we will sue you,'* take legal advice straightaway. Don't be bullied into paying your money to someone without a fight just because they sound impressive, or threaten you. If it happens, say nothing, admit nothing and then see your lawyer.

If you hesitate to ask for your money you risk losing it. Go to the debtor's premises if necessary because unless there is a genuine dispute, if they haven't paid by 120 days, loss – possibly total loss – is highly likely. If there is a genuine dispute or other issue, fix it because then it can't remain a non-payment excuse. If a customer goes broke before you get paid, odds are you will never see your money, or if you do it will only be a percentage; usually a very small one. If you suspect that a customer is in difficulties, especially one who owes you a lot, ask for payment straightaway.

Large companies with sound systems get their credit staff to make friendly phone calls to debtors before due date. This is to see if there are any queries and if the invoices are in the payment system and whether the account will be paid on time, and if not why not. In small businesses without credit staff doing this is time-consuming, but doing it for your top few big accounts can be enjoyable as it speeds up payment!

If you enjoy getting paid be decisive. Ask debtors to pay within a week of it being overdue – this book shows how. Go to their premises to collect it if necessary as it could save the drama and cost of bringing in the heavies.

ACTION PLAN.

Reduce your bad debt risk right now because there may be little or no warning of impending loss. You can get paid by having a basic system.

BAD DEBT RISK MANAGEMENT PLAN

I will do credit checks before opening accounts;   Yes ☐

I will credit check big customers if they pay late
or give me reasons for concern;   Yes ☐

I will contact those who owe heaps before due
date for reasons in this chapter   Yes ☐
and will do so by:
Phone   ☐
Email   ☐
Fax   ☐

I will contact overdue debtors on the _____ (i.e. 4th) day after payment was due
By phone ☐
By email ☐
By fax ☐

I will follow them up on the _____ (i.e. 7th) day)
By phone ☐
By email ☐
By fax ☐

I will then do the following (after reading this book)
1 _____
2 _____
3 _____

WHAT IS CREDIT CONTROL?

Credit control done properly is a customer-relations, sales building and problem solving tool. This can make you, or your staff, feel good about asking for money and change a chore into a joy, so it has more benefits than just getting the money in.

Credit control is also your early warning system of customer complaints. '*I'm not paying you because...*' can signal a complaint and let you fix the problem before losing the customer.

The methods shown in this book are non-aggressive and obtain payment without upsetting customers, because as well as getting paid you just might want them to buy from you again ...

Debt collection on the other hand is the extermination of a relationship, so when asking customers to pay, avoid acting like a dictator or a thug because credit control is not debt collecting.

The Concise Oxford Dictionary defines *credit* as: *A good reputation; belief or trust; a person's financial standing; the sum of money at a person's disposal in a bank; the power to obtain goods etc. before payment (based on the trust that payment will be made); reputation for solvency and honesty in business.* This sums it up – the trust, or hope, you will get paid. Credit is both a business and a personal necessity. There are few of us who do not owe someone something, whether on a mortgage, a credit card or the electricity bill.

Business credit was once only granted as a convenience to those who did not really need it. It was given because it was more practical for regular customers to pay for goods at 30 days rather than upon collection. This was in the days of, *My word is my bond,* but it did not stop bad debts and to reduce this risk Dun & Bradstreet started what is probably the world's first credit checking service in New York during the 1840s. Granting credit needs a wide knowledge of business and a good understanding of human nature.

There is nothing new under the sun. Greek and Roman records show that bad debts and people who *did a runner* were problems several thousand years ago. In pre-Victorian England, specialised debtors prisons held those who did not run far enough. If bad debtors were to be locked up today, a very big jail would be needed. Limited liability companies and trusts protect the personal assets of many bad debtors. Wilful bad debtors, however, are similar to shoplifters, but unlike shoplifters, they are not usually prosecuted as criminals.

Today, the title of *credit controller* is given to the person in charge of getting customers to pay. Big companies employ them because they have large numbers of debtors. Small firms usually have too few debtors to justify a specialist credit controller, or an accounts department.

In smaller businesses, credit control is often done by the office person, sales team or the owners – when they have time, that is. Back-office chores are non-core activities and they do not create sales so it is tempting to pass the credit control buck. But if you do your bank account will suffer.

The *Selecting your credit controller* chapter shows how to overcome buck-passing and even if you cannot turn credit control into a joy, it can at least be satisfying. If your credit terms are payment at 30 days or end of month, with good credit control your debtors aging should be at least as good as this:

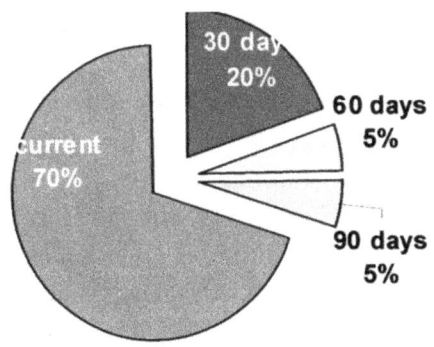

Ideal Aged Debtors

If you give 30 day or end of month terms, at least 70% of the money owed to you should be due on the 30th of the current month (which means it is not overdue). Ideally nothing should be overdue, but as it's not a perfect world, no more than 20% should be 30 days overdue and no more 5% should be at 60 days and a maximum 5% at 90 days. Sound reasons, and not excuses, are needed for

60 and 90 day overdue accounts; such as extended terms agreed *before making the sale and not afterwards*! If there is a dispute or a defect in the goods or services, these should have been rectified as soon as possible to preserve customer relationships and to obtain payment. If your debtors aging is as good, or better, than the above you are controlling your debtors instead of them controlling you. Good credit control helps you beat the above, but if your aging is worse your cashflow suffers and bad debt risk escalates.

Although there is a trend (by big businesses in particular) to reduce payment terms from 30 days to 14 days, or less, to improve their cashflow and bad debt risk, not all businesses can do this, especially small ones. In tough times, prompt payment discounts can be an incentive, but they can cause more problems than they solve. They have to be large to be effective - 2.5% is usually too small and 10% can be too expensive, but does stand a better chance of working. Customers who fail to pay on time can become resentful and be tempted to deduct the discount even when paying late. Big customers could use their clout to negotiate a discount whilst still retaining their previous payment habits, or agree to improvements then revert to bad habits as soon as they can.

When to close a customer's account for non-payment depends on circumstances that are looked at later. Stopping their credit, or withholding supply, involves assessing your situation and theirs – especially their ability to pay at all! If they are just going through a temporary hard time, threatening to close their account can change the customer's attitude from; *I want to pay, but can't just yet,* to *I won't pay you for ages if you close my account!*

There is a comparison between how to treat your debtors and how an auditor treats their clients' staff. An auditor is a watchdog and not a bloodhound and they are careful to treat clients' staff with respect, because failure to do so can result in a change of auditors at the next shareholder meeting. Failure to treat your debtors with respect can cause them to stop buying from you and they won't wait until a meeting. By all means be a watchdog but let debt collectors be bloodhounds. A diligent watchdog avoids the need for bloodhounds and gets the money in and maintains, or even improves, customer relationships.

If the reason they have not paid is shortage of money, ask them what is causing it. If it because business is so bad they are about to go bust, then visit them right away to see if you can get paid. If they are too far away, do your best to get paid by phone because a chat can be more effective than emails and use the methods in the last few chapters of this book. If the reason for non-payment is that they also have overdue accounts, then offering to help them get paid can get you paid too. Even if you do not have a trained credit controller and you, or your staff, are the ones who ask for money, offering help will tell you if it is just an excuse – if it is genuine buy them a copy of this book as a thank you for paying you! Even if you cannot do much to help it generates goodwill, and that as shown later, puts you close to the top of the payment queue. Helping customers this way has changed credit control from debt collecting to customer relations building. The next step is selling.

THE CREDIT CONTROL AND SALES SKILLS ADVANTAGE

Credit Control has evolved in progressive companies from just chasing money to getting new business as well.

Once upon a time credit controllers were not allowed to mix with *good* customers in case they annoyed them. This was in 'the dragon in the cave age' – only let the dragon out when you wanted to scare them into paying. After that you crossed your fingers and hoped they remained customers because credit control was like flame throwing. Old-fashioned credit control was like debt collecting – pay up or else.

Today, credit control is a relationship building skill. It is non-aggressive, yet assertive. The objective is to turn the overdue account into a priority payment in your customer's eye – they need to pay you before paying others because it is to their advantage. What advantages you can offer? – Free or reduced price consultation, priority service option, special price as a thankyou for their business (and for paying) or other applicable incentive? **Write your ideas in the margin right now so you don't forget them - if they result in a new sale provided they pay, your credit control has become a sales tool.**

Credit staff rarely think they are sales people. *I'm too abrasive to sell,* or *Selling is not my strong point,* are common reactions. Yet the personality that makes a good credit controller can make a good sale person. Both jobs involve contact with people. Both use persuasion to get results - either payment or a new order.

Some companies have combined the two into one. For example, Pepsi UK turned their credit controllers into credit reps. It turned out that most of their controllers, who thought they were poor at sales, became good at both and found their jobs more interesting. The advantage of combining credit control and sales was an improvement in efficiency. Fewer staff were needed, sales rose and bad debts dropped. If you, or an employee, have a credit control background, take advantage of these negotiation skills and see if your other people have the skills too.

But hesitate before asking the sales team to do credit control as sales people often hate asking for money. Getting sales is their job, and asking for money for previous sales can be unpleasant and against their nature. If sales people are asked to do credit control, they are unlikely to be enthusiastic and may only make a half-hearted attempt. If you have to get them to ask for money, give them a copy of this book as it is hard for them to ask for yesterday's money in one breath, then trying to get today's sales in the next. But it may not be that hard for your credit controller to do so, depending on what you sell.

CREDIT CONTROL v DEBT COLLECTION

Some people do not know the difference between two. This is understandable for a small business owner or a person with no formal business qualifications, but some people who should know the difference sometimes do not. You may come across some professionally qualified people who still think credit control and debt collecting are the same.

THE DIFFERENCE IS:
Credit control is a customer relationship building tool.
Debt collection is relationship death.

The credit control systems in this book are designed to manage trade credit for businesses selling to other businesses. Before a new account is opened, prudent suppliers do a credit check, allocate a credit limit and get new customers to sign their terms and conditions of trade, and ideally although infrequently, a personal guarantee. Unless other terms have been arranged, such as payment at 7 days, payment is usually due at 30 days, or at the end of the following month (this varies and in New Zealand it is usually 20th of the following month) and well-organised credit control keeps the system on the rails.

One reason for slow payment is reluctance to ask for money, which is especially true for smaller businesses and professional firms. These days, the *only-pay-when-asked* strategy is common and some advisors and bankers tell their clients to operate in this way. This is unethical because if businesses buy goods or services on credit they should pay for them on due date – or receive payment if they are the seller. But even the best intentioned businesses sometimes defer payment because they can't afford to pay just yet, which is why credit control is needed.

Doing credit checks before opening new accounts reduces the risk of your money going down the drain. Try and get a personal guarantee if they are a limited company or a limited partnership – see the *Before you begin* chapter.

If your debtors are good as or better than the previous pie chart you are controlling them. If not, then effective credit control will do wonders for your business and bank balance - it might even save you from going broke …

ACTION PLAN – This is how and why I will quickly get paid:

Effective credit control will fix these problems;

1 _____
2 _____
3 _____

I will get paid these ways;

1 _____
2 _____
3 _____

Credit control will be done by; (name(s))

1 _____
2 _____

If we can't do the above, other options are;
(see *Outsourcing, factoring and other options* chapter)

_____
_____
_____
_____
_____
_____

CREDIT CHECKING

Credit checks reduce late payment and bad debt risks. But to achieve this they need doing **before granting credit** and not left until your customer (client if you wish) is in arrear and owes you heaps. A basic check is easy and only takes 10 to 15 minutes for customers with a good, or acceptable, payment record. When the amount of credit is substantial (meaning non-payment could bankrupt you) in-depth checks are needed, which take longer but can save you from losing your shirt, skirt or much more.

If you are worried about existing customers who are in arrear and owe you heaps, then at least do a quick credit check on them too. If they are in a risky sector, such as construction, speculative or other risky enterprise, do an in-depth check. Also do one if they ask for big increases in credit or run into trouble (or look as though they could). This even applies to long-standing customers because long-standing does not mean they can't go broke …

For new customers, the depth of check depends upon the amount of credit requested and the default risk. For small amounts a few minutes making two to four calls can be enough to make a decision. For more substantial accounts, an in-depth check is needed and a rule of thumb on the difference between the two is:

If they fail to pay, what affect will it have on our business? If it will harm or bankrupt us we must do a detailed check.

BASIC CREDIT CHECKS

Get new customers to complete a credit application form (an example is in chapter 7) if you do not have one. Even if you do have one, insert an extra line for **four** credit references instead of the standard **thee** most credit application forms have. The reason is that skilful slow-payers often pay three creditors on time and use them as credit references. These types pay their other creditors much later.

Start by phoning the fourth reference first because that might be the only call needed to decline credit and save payment hassles, or a bad debt. But before declining their application find out if their poor record is because of a once-only dispute or other valid reason. If there are frequent payment or dispute problems with this customer either they are a bad credit risk or the supplier you phoned sells lousy goods or services. To find out, phone the next referee – it could be fun!

If instead of problems the fourth reference's comments show a reasonable payment record *(defined as they usually pay on time and if they pay late it is rarely more than two weeks late)*, then phone the third referee, then the second and finally the first. Doing it in reverse order is quicker because you might not need to make four calls to make a *no* decision if their record is poor. But before making a *yes* decision, try and phone all four and definitely do so if you encounter an adverse comment to see if that is only a blip, or something worse. If their record is poor, decline the application and to make it sweeter, offer a cash discount instead.

When doing credit checks, speak to the supplier's credit controller, if they have one. If they do not, speak to whoever can help, which in a small firm might be the owner. It is now a bit harder to do credit checks than it once was because some businesses ask whether you have the customer's permission. Our credit application form provides this and if yours does not, you can use our wording unless there are specific requirements in your state.

If you phone someone who is uncooperative (fortunately a minority), say something like, *'Oh, don't YOU do credit checks then?'* or better still, *'Your customer gave us your name as a reference. Surely you want to help your customers, don't you?'* to see if that breaks the ice. If it fails to and if this referee is important to your decision say; *'I will tell your customer that the reason we cannot grant them credit is because of **your** unwillingness to help!'* This almost always persuades them to cooperate. If it does not you still have another three referees, unless you strike it unlucky with them too, which would be unusual.

TO DO A QUICK CHECK, JUST ASK:
"Do they pay their account more or less on time, or are they a pain?"

Saying the above tells you most you need to know. They can say *yes, no* or *sometimes* and it saves a lot of fuss. As almost all businesses have occasionally paid late, it lets you know whether they are good, bad or fair.

You might encounter a few bureaucratic businesses who demand written requests before making credit worthiness comments and if you do then use something like the following:

ON YOUR LETTERHEAD

Date

To

Attention:

Re: (Name of your proposed customer in bold)

The above has requested a credit facility with us and has given permission to approach you for a credit reference. We would be grateful if you could tell us the following either by phoning me on _____ (your number) or by email, fax or mail as above.

1. Length of time they have been credit account customers _____ months/years (please circle one)
2. Frequency of purchases _____ every monthly, quarterly or irregular (circle one)
3. What is their average monthly spend or spend per order? $_____ (approx)
4. Their credit limit (if any) is $_____ Do they exceed it? Yes, sometimes, no (circle one)
5. Your payment terms for this customer are _____ 7 days, end of month, other (circle one)
6. How is their payment performance? Excellent   Good   Acceptable Poor (circle one)

We hope to be of similar service to you and thank you for your kind assistance.

Yours sincerely,

Fax or email the above then phone to prompt them either to quickly complete it – or ideally to get a verbal reference by asking the, *'Do they pay you more or less on time, or are they a pain?'* question.

IN-DEPTH CHECKS

In-depth credit checks take longer but are vital if large sums are involved and late payment or a default would damage or bankrupt you. In such cases, it could be prudent to approach a credit rating or assessment firm, such as Dun & Bradstreet, Veda (examples only and not endorsements or recommendations) or others who specialise in this. Their fees are worth it because it could save you from serious problems and sleepless nights. But to save you an unnecessary cost, first do the following:

1. Do the basic credit check. If this raises doubts over their payment record, or their level of disputes and their ability to pay, these could be reasons to decline the credit request so no further check, or expense, will be needed.
2. If step 1 is satisfactory, now is the time to obtain a credit rating agency report which should tell you enough to make a decision. Reports can be quickly obtained from good agencies (they know the need for speed) if your prospective customer is big enough or been around long enough to have been assessed. If they are not

big or are new, the question will be; *Why does this small or new outfit want so much credit?*

If they are too small or too new to have a credit rating file and you want their business, then obtain personal guarantees from the directors, shareholders or other officers and depending on the amount involved possibly other security too. Personal guarantees are not worth much if the guarantors have few assets and you will not know if the family homes and beachfront properties are owned by a trust, or mortgaged unless your lawyer does a search. Liens and second or third mortgages could be worthless, so discuss it with your lawyer or accountant.

If you have, or will have, a lot of money tied up in debtors or otherwise invested in your business, speak to your lawyer and accountant regarding all forms of business risks and ways of protecting your personal assets if the business fails and/or if legal actions are taken against you. When it comes to debtors, use this extension of the previous rule of thumb as a guide:

What would happen to me and my family if a big customer failed to pay? What would happen if my top three customers all failed to pay?

Write what will or could happen here _____

_____

_____

_____

SCARY CREDIT

Your credit checks have checked out reasonably OK, so you open a 30 day account with a $4,000 limit, which is about a month's sales. They pay promptly the first month and you are thrilled when next month's order is $8,000 even though it is double the credit limit. This time they pay a week late, which you overlook. In month three they place a $12,000 order, which is three times the credit limit, and say that because your service and quality are great they will buy even more in future, so will you increase the credit limit to $15,000? You agree, but they pay two weeks late this time, which again you overlook as you and your staff are busy. Monthly sales increase to $15,000, but payment slips a week each month and you have to phone several times to get paid. They apologise and say their business is growing so fast staff can barely cope, but they are employing more to fix it.

They pay $8,000 in good faith and say they will be current next month, but they still owe $45,000, which is triple their new limit and over 11 times the original $4,000. You decide to limit your exposure to $45,000 until after you have done another credit check, but you continue to supply on a cash-with-order basis to keep their custom, goodwill and an incentive to pay you. You also ask for a $10,000 weekly payment until their account is current. They agree and say they will definitely pay all the arrears in a month or so, but ask to pay for current purchases weekly because they use online banking and cannot pay cash with each order. You agree and they buy $10,000 that week, but forget to pay, so they now owe $55,000.

You phone their credit references, starting with the fourth, then the rest. With each call you get more worried. At the end you are terrified - they've just gone broke and now you could too.

You wake up in a sweat. It is 3.30am and can't get back to sleep. You hope it's only a dream because if they owe $55,000 you have a living nightmare. You go to work early to find out how much they really owe because your accounts are behind and everyone's too busy to do credit control, so it could be even more than you think. You double check and find that it was just a bad dream because they only owe $6,000, but it's a month overdue and is 50% more than their credit limit. You reach for your copy of Get paid! to fix things before it gets out of hand. It was only a dream and they haven't gone broke, but the reason they cannot pay is because their customers are not paying. You buy an extra copy of Get paid! to give to them because they are growing rapidly and they could become a $15,000 a month customer as they do say you and your products are really good!

To prevent anymore nasty dreams you fix your accounts and credit control problems. You also get new terms of trade instead of using pirated copies from your rivals, and get all new and existing customers to sign them - this was easier than you feared because you gave an incentive discount for their next service. Because you couldn't get personal guarantees from the directors of your biggest debtors, you discretely enforced credit limits to prevent their accounts from becoming liabilities that could bankrupt you. As an unsecured creditor, which is what you are, you are at the bottom of the pile when it comes to getting paid when a business collapses. The only ones lower down are the shareholders.

Becoming a secured creditor is hard for trade creditors and is almost the exclusive preserve of banks and other lenders because it involves debentures and other securities that have to be registered. Whilst it is unusual for trade creditors to obtain securities as strong as those of banks, it is not totally impossible. If the debtor really needs your support, they could be willing to give you some security, so speak to your accountant for a solution.

Few businesses have the nerve to ask for securities and personal guarantees, but if you don't ask you will never get … Better to ask and be told *no* than not to ask at all – they will at least respect you for being business-like and may sign a personal guarantee or other security.

ACTION PLAN – My quick checklist before granting credit is:

We will do credit checks before opening accounts   Yes ☐ No ☐ If No, why?

We will get new customers to sign account application forms, including terms of trade, **before granting credit.**   Yes ☐ and will then:

- Check credit references *before giving credit* – *do the last one first;*
- Try and get personal guarantees - insist or speak to your accountant if purchases will be significant;
- Get professional credit checks on customers whose default could cripple or destroy you. This includes **existing customers** who place significant orders.

The person(s) who will do credit checks are:

1 _____

2 _____

SELECTING YOUR CREDIT CONTROLLER

Getting paid without being aggressive is easy if you have a good credit controller who knows how to handle slow-payers without upsetting them. If you do not employ credit staff, appoint the most suitable person for the job, just the same as you would for any other position. Because your success, or survival, hinges on it, don't pass credit control off to a scapegoat.

These questions help choose the most suitable person:

Do they have time? If not, what other tasks can you spare them from?

Do they have the personality to ask customers for money? Some people hate it and can be on the back-foot, become stressed, aggressive or apologetic.

Are they a good negotiator? If not, buy them a copy of this book so they can make personalized notes in it to improve their skills.

Credit control is an admin job and in small businesses admin is usually handled by one person. If this applies to your business and there isn't the time to do everything, some things will simply not be done. People quit if they are stressed or overworked - or take out a claim against you.

If you have nobody suitable, or their other duties are too valuable but you have problems getting paid, read the *Outsourcing, factoring & other options* chapter. If you have end-of-month terms and 50 debtors, credit control can take a day or more a month, but inconveniently spread out. If you have 7 or 14 day terms, it can take twice as long. Pro rata the time needed based on the number of debtors and who you sell to as some sectors are slow-paying, others are faster.

SABOTAGING YOUR CREDIT CONTROL

If you have selected the right person, give them the authority to do the job – total authority and don't meddle. If you outsource it to a professional outfit, they will know what to do and guide you on credit policy, plus what to do when slow payers ask for extra time.

Meddling is a sure way of sabotaging your credit control, especially by making *special arrangements* with pet customers when their account is overdue. Doing this is demoralising and risky, so consult your credit controller first - she might know more about the customer than you do; such as they are about to go broke! More bad debts are incurred with pet customers, friends and relatives than is realised, so being at arms-length to all customers when it comes to credit is businesslike - if they are a relative or friend, they should pay you first! To get out of jams when overdue debtors ask for extra time, say something like this:

"We employ a credit controller and it is against our policy to make special arrangements with anybody without consulting him/her."

If you are a small business where you are the boss and credit controller, blame the policy on the bank, the accountant, shareholders, partners or anybody else who comes to mind - *write your scapegoat in the margin right now!*

Unless you have lots of debtors, make one person responsible for credit control. Sharing it can mean that nobody takes responsibility, so if you need to give it to more than one, give each a specific number of accounts (for example, debtors A-M to person one and N-Z to person two), or some other way of distributing the work so that staff are accountable and buck-passing avoided. Accountability works both ways – don't interfere if they are doing a good job. If they are doing well but a few customers' feathers are ruffled because they are a bit abrasive, buy them a copy of this book so they can adjust their style without losing effectiveness.

Although not usually recommended as good practice, your credit controller may need to negotiate part payment or other terms to get your money. This may need doing on the spot, so give them guidelines on what they can and cannot do. If they are uncertain they can say, *"I will have to discuss it and phone you back."* If you are the boss and credit controller, say you have to seek approval from the bank, the accountant or the scapegoat guy you wrote in the margin.

If you decide to accept part-payments, get them to pay the first one today if possible, or definitely this week and not next month, otherwise they are getting you off their back and receiving an extra month's credit before paying a cent!

As the longer a debt is overdue the greater the default risk, be careful about extended part payments. Get weekly amounts and if they promise to pay by online banking but renege more than once, insist on post-dated cheques (*cheques* are spelt *checks* in the US but the UK, Australian, NZ, South African etc spelling of *cheques* is used throughout to save confusion). The reason for post dated cheques is it means they have accepted the fact they owe the money and issuing cheques makes it hard for them to dispute the debt later. Tell them if they really are in a jam when the cheques are due, they can ask you to delay banking them. If they take you up on this, ask them very probing questions before agreeing.

Depending on the number of debtors and the amounts outstanding, consider sending your credit staff, or yourself, to a one-day credit control seminar. This can save lots of time and money, so do a web search by entering *credit control seminars in* (your location) or similar.

ACTION PLAN – deciding now will save you pain later.

The person(s) who will do credit control are

1 _____

2 _____

3 _____

Will I consider outsourcing? YES ☐ NO ☐ Maybe ☐ Reasons:

_____

_____

Can I/staff benefit from a credit control seminar? YES ☐ NO ☐
Maybe ☐ Reasons:

_____

_____

_____

OUTSOURCING, FACTORING AND OTHER OPTIONS

If you do not have credit control or other staff who can ask for money, or you can't afford to carry your debtors even if they pay more or less on time, look at the following get-paid options. If the problem is lack of staff and time, outsourcing could solve your problem. If you are short of working capital, look at factoring, but get professional advice as shown later on before jumping in because the factoring pond can be treacherous.

OUTSOURCE DEBTOR MANAGEMENT

If it's all too hard and you don't have the staff or time, then outsource your credit control, or your entire debtor management. Outsourcing is ideal for tightly run, short-staffed businesses and can be cheaper than managing debtors in-house.

Really professional outsource credit control and debtor management specialists act like a member of your staff without being on your payroll. Your debtors need not know they are involved because everything can be done in your name. Outsourcing can put you at the top of payment queues, so you get paid first. Not being at the top means getting paid late, often after all the rest. In tough times, getting paid and lowering costs is vital to survival, so look closely at outsourcing as it can achieve both.

Getting tomorrow's business today instead of chasing yesterday's money tomorrow could be your cheapest and best option. Businesses with few staff sometimes ask relatives or friends to do credit control, but if this is not a good idea, then should you do it? You can, but should you? Your time is probably worth more than your charge-out rate, so if you are busy, use it to grow your business instead of chasing money. Whilst credit control is essential it is a non-earning task, so if you lack the time, or staff and have payment problems, outsourcing can fix it.

If you have problems invoicing-out on time, outsourcing can fix that too, especially if you charge by time, quotation, time and materials, time and travel and other non-inventory or low-inventory businesses. Late invoicing can be a problem for some professionals, such as IT support, accountants (it's true!), lawyers, surveyors, contract engineers, public relations/advertising agents, farm vets, trades people and lots of others. If you suffer from this problem, chances are you get paid late and have less cash than you otherwise could. That's avoidable and fixing it will make being in business much more fun!

If you don't fit into the above, you could at least benefit from outsourcing your credit control and perhaps outsource invoicing too if you are a contractor, fabricator, assembler, panel beater, sand blaster, plumber, electrician, landscaper, interior designer or other business where invoicing is reasonably straightforward

It is pointless pretending your invoicing is up-to-date by backdating them, such as dating them 31 March when it is really 10 April. If the invoice hasn't been received on time, they will not pay on 30 April when *you* think it is due, but on 31 May, when *they* think it is due. Many businesses close-off their books soon after month end and if your invoice is not received on time it will not be paid according to your timescale, simple as that. If your invoices are mailed, your customers will probably date stamp them on receipt and if they are emailed, the transmission date is a dead giveaway! Ask customers when their close-off dates are and ensure your invoices are received before then. If this is too hard, outsource it or get help from family or others.

The reason why outsourcing is successful is because it improves efficiency and reduces costs. Its future depends on these and if it fails to deliver, outsourcing will be a passing fad. Outsource credit control can reduce costs, such as wages, and cash flow improvements can reduce interest costs and bad debt risk. Efficiency gains can also be made by freeing-up your time and that of key staff.

Outsourcing has existed for well over a century and examples are recruitment and insurance broking. Recruiters, brokers and advertising agencies are so well established they are no longer regarded as outsource providers, but the fact is they are. To a degree, auditing is a form of outsourcing and can be mandatory.

Outsource credit control started in USA and then spread to UK, Canada, Australia, New Zealand and other countries. Originally, the factoring companies had the largest market share, but was tied to their factoring products (see next section) and is not suitable for all businesses. There are now outsource debtor management providers other than factors that specialise in small to medium size enterprises, which is where the demand and need is. Do an online search by entering key words, such as, *accounts receivable solutions, credit control, debtor management* or *outsource credit control* and similar phrases into a search engine to see what is available locally. It might also dredge-up some debt collectors, which unless they really have something special and customer friendly - at time of writing none seem to do - ignore them unless you need a debt collector. If there are no local outsourcers, then distance might not be a problem for you or them these days.

FACTORING

Factoring by its critics is called borrowing of last resort. By its supporters it is regarded as an excellent, if expensive, source of working capital. The points in its favour are that the factor should advance up to 90% of the money owed by your debtors within days of the sale. Then, instead of the debtor paying you they pay the factor in accordance with your normal terms of trade and when they do the factor pays you the 10% balance, less a commission of two to four percent. This unfortunately means you are giving the factor two to four percent of your gross margin. You have to work out whether you can afford this, or if it is worth it.

Factoring is normally more expensive than borrowing from the bank, but can be less than the merchant fees of some credit card companies.

To protect themselves from fraud, before the factor advances you the money they contact your customers to verify that the sales are genuine. Whilst you would never write false invoices and then try and get the factor to pay you 90% of the value, as that would be fraud and not nice, it has happened. The factor will also tell the debtor that payment must be made directly to them and not to you as you cannot have your cake and eat it.

Before deciding to factor, get full disclosures (the warts and all stuff) from them on what their requirements are. This includes details of any guarantees and other securities they want from you, what their credit control methods are, when will they advance the money, how much will they advance, what their charges are and when will they ask for their money back if your customer does not pay them – this is known as recourse and many factoring outfits insist on it. Those that do not (*non recourse*) charge more as their risks are higher, but it can be much safer for you. **But if you do not have a financial background, don't sign anything until speaking to your accountant or other knowledgeable person.** You could speak to your bank and their advice should be free, but some factoring companies are owned by banks. Find out from the factor who owns them in case it is your bank, and if it is you might not get impartial advice. Although the benefit of factoring is that you get most of your money within a few days, which can fix your cash flow problems, it is not normally a cheap solution.

Besides cost, there can be other issues with factoring, such as long term contracts, personal guarantees and, as mentioned, recourse. Some want long-term contracts and insist that all credit sales are channelled through them. Shop around as not all insist on contracts and some will let you pick and chose which debtors to factor. If the factor wants a personal guarantee, think hard and take professional advice before giving one and search for one that does not insist on it.

The problem with recourse is that if the debtor does not pay the factor, they direct debit your account with the amount advanced. You will then be hit with an unplanned withdrawal and this could be a big amount, which is why the factor wants the personal guarantee in case the direct debit bounces. If it does and you have signed a personal guarantee you could lose your home and be bankrupted. While the factor will, or should have, an in-house credit control team, you have no control over their performance or methods. These are reasons for refusing to give a personal guarantee because, like you, the factor is in business and they, like you, should accept the commercial risks involved. It would though be reasonable for them to require a fidelity guarantee to protect them if you did-a-runner, but get the wording checked by your lawyer before signing.

Factoring firms can be found in search engines or similar and are often under *Finance—factoring, invoice discounting* or similar.

OTHER FINANCE

Some banks have factor-like products that are cheaper (so they say) and more user-friendly insofar as not insisting on personal guarantees. But they will need their normal securities and probably require a fidelity guarantee in case you take their money and run. Whilst banks call these products by different names, such as invoice or debtor finance, very few will do your credit control and they regard the facility as sort of term loan and leave the credit control to you, which means that debtors pay you in the normal manner, but the money has to go into an account specified by the bank. Not all banks offer the facility and some of those that do are only interested in businesses with credit sales of more than $4million a year, which prevents small businesses from using it. Because lending criteria changes, as do bank products and services, contact various banks to see what they offer. If one has a product suitable to you but you do not bank with them, naturally you will have to open an account and perhaps make it your main or sole account, but you won't know unless you ask!

Ask your accountant to keep you informed of other debtor or invoice financing products that have newly been introduced because they should know about them through their professional journals and other sources. If you don't have an accountant, approach some to see if they will keep you informed - they probably will because you are a potential clients at some stage. Unless you ask them to research it for you, there should be no charge for passing information to you as it is part of normal client relationship management. If they do charge, find another accountant ...

Whatever you decide, never go-easy on asking customers to pay. It doesn't cost a lot to shepherd your debtors - it can save you from going broke too.

ACTION PLAN - doing the following could fix my problems.

What to do about my debtors

1. Who does our credit control?   Credit controller ☐
   Accounts staff ☐
   Me ☐
   Nobody until we are short of money ☐

2. Is our debtor aging as good as the chart in chapter 3?   Yes ☐   No ☐

3. Are we short of money?   Often ☐   Occasionally ☐   Rarely ☐

4. Do I/my staff find it hard to ask for money?   Yes ☐   No ☐

5. Are we good at asking for money?   Yes ☐   No ☐

6. Is my time/staff time effectively used for debtor mgt?   Yes ☐   No ☐
   If not, why not? _____
   _____

7. Could we benefit from outsource credit control?   Yes ☐   No ☐
   Reasons _____
   _____

8. Could we benefit from other outsource invoicing etc? Yes ☐   No ☐
   Reasons _____
   _____

9. Could I benefit from factoring/invoice finance?   Yes☐   No ☐
   Reasons _____
   _____

10. I will approach the banks to see what they have got.   Yes ☐   No ☐
    If Yes, when .... (date) If No, why not? _____
    _____

11. Will I ask my/an accountant to keep me informed? Yes ☐ No ☐

   Reasons if No _____

   _____

12. If I do not have an accountant, do I need one? Yes ☐ No ☐

   Unless it is lack of money, reasons if No _____

   _____

13 If the above does not solve my problems, other solution are_____

   _____

   _____

   _____

BEFORE YOU BEGIN

Beware of cash sale customers who suddenly want credit as they are a bad debt risk if the reason is they can't pay cash … Whilst they are unlikely to say they are short of money, find out the real reason. If you cannot or it is unsatisfactory, decline the request, or failing that impose a credit limit (a small one that would not damage you if they defaulted) and weekly payment terms. Even if they have been customers for a long time, this will probably be the first time they have bought on credit, so get them to complete a credit application form and do credit checks as shown in the Credit Checking chapter. If you do not have credit application forms, use the one overleaf.

Credit checking takes some of the gamble out of the getting-paid game, so get all new customers (including cash sale customers requesting credit) to complete a credit application form and do a credit check before opening the account. Up-to-date terms of trade (see *Terms & conditions of trade* chapter), signed by customers, plus personal guarantees also help protect you. Too few businesses have the nerve to ask for personal guarantees, but if you don't ask you will never get. Better to ask and be told *'no'* than not ask at all. They should at least respect you for being business-like and may sign the guarantee - insist if purchases will be substantial and default would cripple you, or worse.

The above reduces the need for debt collection, which is inconvenient at the least and costly if the debtor is hard to trace, which is why the credit application form needs to contain the directors or partners residential addresses. Even when debt collection works, it destroys customer relationships, often forever (see Let's go a-courting chapter), so use effective credit control instead (or outsource it) to reduce or eliminate the need for debt collection. Keep records and invoicing up-to-date because, as mentioned in Chapter 6, failing to do so puts you on crutches.

Credit Application Form. *Notice. The following forms are examples only and the publishers and author do not accept any liability for their usage under any circumstances. Legal advice is needed to ensure that all your documentation is in accordance with the needs of your business and the laws and precedents of your jurisdiction.*

CREDIT APPLICATION

Legal name of business _____ Date established _____

Trading name if different _____ ABN/ACN _____

Street address _____

Delivery Address if different _____

Postal address _____

Address of registered office _____

Phone _____ Mobile _____ Fax _____ E-mail _____

What does your business do? _____

Bank and Branch _____ Account No _____

Accountants _____ Solicitor _____

Are you a (please ✓) Company ☐ Partnership ☐ Sole Trader ☐ Other ☐ _____ (describe)

If you are a <u>Sole Trader/Partnership</u> please give details of nearest relative in Australia not living with you:

Name of relative _____ Relationship _____

Address of relative _____

<u>Is the business a partnership, a trust or other body?</u>   Yes ☐ No ☐ If Yes, please complete as follows:

Details of (as applicable): Directors, partners, sole trader or trustees/other principals

1. Full name _____ Phone no. _____

Residential address _____

2. Full name _____ Phone no. _____

Residential address _____

3. Full name _____ Phone no. _____

Residential address _____

(Please list on reverse if more than three)

Amount of credit required per month $ _____ If a company/corp, paid up capital is $_____

Who do we contact in your business for:

Purchasing: Name _____ Email _____

Paying accounts: Name _____ Email _____

Trade References

1. Name _____ Phone No (_____) _____

2. Name _____ Phone No (_____) _____

3. Name _____ Phone No (_____) _____

4. Name _____ Phone No (_____) _____

I/we agree that payment will be made within 30 days of the date of invoice and the supplier reserves the right to charge interest on unpaid accounts at the rate of 5% above the supplier's bank overdraft rate then in force and to fully recover all costs incurred in the collection of this account and any other money owing to the company. I/we agree to abide by the supplier's terms and conditions of trade and as may be varied from time to time and hereby acknowledge that ownership of all goods or services supplied remains with the supplier until they and all other moneys outstanding have been paid in full. I/we authorise any person or company to provide the supplier with any information that may be required at any time with regard to this application and my/our credit worthiness.

Applicants name _____ Position _____

Applicants signature _____ Date _____

TERMS AND CONDITIONS ARE ALSO REQUIRED TO BE SIGNED

TERMS OF TRADE

Easy-to-follow Terms of Trade samples are in the *Terms & conditions of trade* chapter.

Ideally, Terms of Trade should be attached to the Credit Application form and also be signed by customer. Doing this makes it hard for them to find wriggling-out-of-paying excuses down the track, provided there are no genuine reasons for not paying. If you don't have any Terms of Trade, or have copied those of other businesses (naughty, naughty), or they are out-of-date, ask your lawyer to compile new ones - they might have a suitable low-cost template. Templates can be found in web searches, but check they are suitable and comply with any usage conditions. Terms of trade need looking at occasionally because legislation and court cases can make them obsolete, so phone your lawyer or accountant occasionally to see what's new. Keeping the call to less than six minutes might avoid charges.

PERSONAL GUARANTEES

Bold businesses request *personal guarantees* from company directors or shareholders and those in easy-to-wriggle-out-of partnerships. Once-upon-a-time they were not necessary for sole traders and partnerships because they had (still theoretically have) a personal liability to pay, but their lawyers may have ring-fenced their personal assets and you are unlikely to know this.

For guarantees to be fully enforceable they need to be properly signed and witnessed, so unless you have the qualifications, get them drawn-up by a lawyer - copying someone else's is naughty and they might not be watertight either. To reduce the chances of the so-and-so's later claiming they were signed under duress by saying, *'it was like having a gun pointed at us and we needed the goods right away to stop horrible things happening, so we signed'* or other excuses to invalidate them, it needs to be made clear they are entering into a commitment, which is why a lawyer is needed.

Before tossing guarantees aside as too hard, the good news is that the fact a guarantee has been signed is a strong incentive for the debtor to pay before horrible things happen to them.

Personal Guarantee* *Notice. The following form is an example only and the publishers and author do not accept any liability for its usage under any circumstances. Legal advice is needed to ensure all your documentation is in accordance with the needs of your business and the laws and precedents of your jurisdiction.*

Guarantee

In consideration of you (*Insert name*) at my request agreeing to supply _____ (the purchaser) with the purpose of its business, I _____ (Full name) occupation _____ of _____ (personal address) hereby unconditionally guarantee the due and punctual payment by the purchaser of all moneys which shall include any interest, collection costs, costs and expenses and any other amounts payable by the purchaser as and when the same shall become due and payable by the purchaser (*insert name*) in respect of goods supplied or services rendered. My liability under this guarantee shall be a continuing guarantee and shall not be discharged or affected by the giving of any time, indulgence, extension or credit, waiver or consent at any time to the purchaser or by any variation, modification, amendment to any agreement in respect of the supply of goods or services by the illegality and invalidity or unenforceability of any agreement relating to the supply of goods or services.

Dated this _____ day of _____ 20 ___

Full name of guarantor _____

Signature _____

In the presence of (full name of witness) _____

Witness signature _____

Witness address _____

Witness occupation _____

SLOW PAYMENT SEASONS

Like leaves dropping off trees, there are slow-payment seasons when payments drop off regardless of the state of the economy, so build them into your credit control plans instead of building them into your cashflow.

The main slow-payment seasons are Christmas, New Year and other holiday periods. Whilst there may be someone around to accept payments, there is rarely anyone there to make them during holidays. Find out when customers will be closing for their breaks because payment delays can increase by 3 weeks or more. If you are owed $40,000, waiting an extra 3 weeks will affect cash flow and interest costs.

If December accounts – or previous arrears - are not paid before Christmas, odds are they will be paid late – in Australia, New Zealand and South Africa it might be late January, and where July/August are the main slow-payment seasons, sometime in September. So contact your debtors, especially those who owe heaps, and get them to pay before they shutdown. If they have not paid, remind them ten days before their closedown, then at five days, two days and on the last day if they still have not paid. There could be other times of the year that payments slow down for your industry, so use the same methods to get paid beforehand.

Other reasons for payment delays include:

- **incorrect pricing;**
- **Despatching the wrong goods or undersupplying;**
- **Order numbers not shown on invoices or not obtained;**
- **Not complying with customers' documentation requirements;**
- **Not adhering to contract terms;**
- **Late invoicing;**
- **Other -** add other reasons applicable to you that can delay payment _____

_____

ACTION PLAN

1. Do I have credit application forms?   Yes ☐   No ☐
2. If Yes are they up-to-date?   Yes ☐   No ☐
(If No to 1 and 2 when will I get them/update them?
                         Now ☐ or by ___ (date)
3. Do I have Terms of Trade?   Yes ☐   No ☐
4. If Yes are they up-to-date?   Yes ☐   No ☐
5. (If No to 3 and 4, when will I get them/update them?
                         Now ☐ or by ___ (date)
6. Is there anything else I can do to get customers to pay on time? _____
_____
_____
_____

HANDS-ON CREDIT CONTROL

Ready, steady go ...

The right frame of mind before starting your credit control helps make it enjoyable and productive and some guidelines are:

1. Be calm - they owe **you** the money and after reading this you can remain calm even if they do not.
2. Build credit control into your schedule twice a week (more if needed) then avoid distractions. By doing this now less time will be needed in future, so it saves time and gets your money.
3. If you have around 25 debtors, two blocks of 20 minutes each week may be all that is needed. If you have 100 debtors two blocks of 80 minutes each could be needed to get paid. The good news is if you do this, less time will be needed in future because debtors will start paying without reminding. The not so good news is that telephone credit control cannot always be done to a set schedule because you can only

speak to customers when they are available and that might not be at the times scheduled by you! In such cases, use email or fax credit control as shown later.

4. Contact big dollar accounts first. This is where most money is tied up and getting paid will do wonders for your bank balance and reduce bad debt risk. Next concentrate on debtors at 90, 60 and 30 days.

5. Avoid being told 'We *paid yesterday*' by checking your mail and bank account. If this is not possible, contact them anyway because they will soon tell you if they have paid ...

6. If your accounts software has a credit control module, using it will save time in the long run. If it does not have a credit control module but you have Customer Relationship Management (CRM) software, try using it for credit control.

7. If your accounts are up to date, print (or print to screen) last month's aged debtors list. If only two or three contacts are needed to obtain payment, writing contact details on the print-out month can work. If it is, say, April use the list at 31 March as it should show the correct aging - aging is wrong on mid-month print-outs in some accounts software. Life is harder if records are behind, but try and enter your invoices and payments received. If you cannot, print out your monthly invoices or use the file copies of invoices and check these off against bank records.

MANUAL RECORDS

If your accounts are behind, or you don't have a credit control module or CRM and only have a few debtors, use the following manual example for credit control. Use lined A4 or foolscap paper and leave several lines between each debtor to write key points at contact. You could write on hard copies of invoices instead, but a list is better as some customers may owe you money on more than one invoice. If you have more than 20 debtors, then acquire accounts software, or outsource your bookkeeping.

Good Service Co
Credit Control :June 2009

Name of debtor   Notes

Poor Payers PL C- $7,500 47 due 31 May 2010

4 June	9.30 am Phoned Mike (accountant) who said they would pay in full today.
6 June	2.15 pm Phoned Mike again - promised to EFT today.
8 June	9.15 am Mike in a meeting. 10.30 Gone to the bank. 12.15. Out for the day.
8 June	12.20 Sent Fax (Remind 1)
9 June	9.15 Phoned, Mike in a meeting 9.20 Faxed Remind 1 again with extra note.
10 June	9.30 Mike at meeting 9.35 Faxed Remind 2 10.15 Mike in another meeting – left message saying he has broken his promise so pay NOW
11 June	**Paid in Full**

I Nerverpay Specialists - $1,790.15 due 31 April 2010

4 June	9.10 Ivor Neverpay says dog ate the invoice again. 9.15 faxed a copy.
4 June	9.20 Ivor says order number not shown. Told him it is shown on top left
5 June	9.05 Sent Remind 3 saying pay in 48 hours or we hand him over
6 June	**Paid In Full**

Shyster & Partners - $2,540.22 due 28 February, 2010

4 June	9.30 Phoned Arch Shyster for 15th time. Told him we will hand him over. Arch says they have no money but might have some next month. Said we will issue winding up order unless he pays now. Arch swore and threatened me. I hung up.
	9.40 Faxed final demand saying winding up action starts in 24 hrs.
6 June	9.15 Told Sue Grabit & Runne to send dummy winding up papers.
8 June	**Paid In Full. Future sales will be cash only or Visa + 2% surcharge.**

When they pay, writing *Paid* with a red pen increases the pleasure. In the days when the only records were paper, cards were often used for recording contacts with each debtor.

ACTION PLAN – if fully prepared put a big tick in the following box.

To get going these need doing _____

_____

_____

_____

_____

_____

TELEPHONE CREDIT CONTROL

*Ask for payment before it's due
to get your money on time.
Then use the following to get it
without even asking …*

If you really want to be effective, instead of waiting until accounts are overdue phone before they are due! This actually reduces the time needed for credit control because you are training customers to pay on time. Once trained, they are more likely to pay without reminders or with just an occasional one to jog their memory. This is how:

If you have monthly terms, phone customers around mid month (or at least big ones) to see if everything is OK. Try and diarise a set day each month – if you need to vary it make it the following day and definitely the same week as that reminds you to do it. It also gets debtors used to your calls and say something like this:

'Good morning Mary, this is Fred the credit controller of Good Service Inc, how are you?' As this is a friendly call and not a demand for money, be relaxed and respond to their comments, but without taking too much time. Next, ask if they have received your invoices (if more than one, list them and check they have got them) and ask if they have been approved and entered into the payment system. If they have not, find out why and either send copies or fix any problems. Doing this overcomes the favourite payment excuses of needing copy invoices or saying, **'We are not paying because....'** Problems or excuses are reasons why calls are better than emails because they enable you to fix things there and then and obtain a payment commitment. Only send emails if you are out of the office as the occasional email can work but calls work better, so call those who owe heaps and if short of time email the smaller ones.

After ascertaining there are no problems (if there are fix them and call back), ask if payment will be made on time. Because you are phoning around two weeks before due date, if they say they are having cashflow problems, you can stop supply right away if they are about to go broke! Most of the time they will say that payment will be made on due date, but if they say it could be late, find out why. If it is because they will be away for awhile, ask if they can pay before going and because few other creditors are likely to be asking this, they might agree.

Getting them to agree to pay on due date overcomes the *only pay when asked attitude* and gives you an advantage if they don't pay. When that happens, phoning to remind them of their promise puts you in a strong position – emails are a poor second and when they fail, call them.

Sending a small thankyou gift to accounts payable people works wonders for credit control. Few businesses do this and if you do it you can get paid when others find it hard, so ask when their birthday is or put them on your Christmas present list. When you know them better, ask how their family is and if the dog has recovered from the bee swarm attack to further strengthen ties. They might then tell you of their employer's problems in advance, such as running out of money or plans to buy from rivals.

Doing the unusual (as long as it is ethical and not a bribe) can put you at the head of payment queues and save time. In the *action plan* at the end of this chapter insert the names of key people, what you will give them (theatre tickets perhaps) and when.

Phone techniques

Reasonable to good negotiating skills are helpful for telephone credit control, but don't fret if you are a bit nervous. They owe the money and it is them who are on the back-foot and not you! If negotiating is not your strongest point, then be a *good* negotiator instead. *Good* in this context means being reasonable and fair and if they are not reasonable and fair in return, the *Abuse* chapter and those following it keep you on the front-foot and turn nervousness into fun. Negotiating gets easier with practice, but is harder if you are dealing with a professional *I Neverpay* (see I Neverpay chapter to turn that into fun too).

The phone is the easiest way of contacting debtors, but drawbacks can be they are out and calls can be soon forgotten or become confrontational, so sometimes an email or a fax is better. If you are experienced in the art of asking for money, or selling or negotiating, you will probably have good phone techniques already. If these are polite, non-aggressive and effective, continue using them. Business-to-business credit control is surprisingly easy as over 90 percent of customers are likely to be friendly - if they are not it is usually easy to make them so and effective methods are:

1. Have details of amount and date due before phoning
2. Relax and be calm so you remain in control
3. Speak to the person who pays the accounts and ask for them by name. If you don't know their name, ask the operator.

The accounts payable person may be a clerk, the accountant, a director or the proprietor. In larger outfits it is good form to start at junior level, then work upwards if they do not pay. In smaller businesses the owner may do everything.

Be polite as you want them to buy from you again and politeness works most of the time, so say something like this:

'Good morning Mary, this is Fred the credit controller of Good Service Inc, how are you?' Pause for their reply and if they ask how you are say you are looking forward to the weekend, and to them paying.

The phrase *how are you* offsets their unease at speaking to credit staff without reducing the impact. Put a bit of empathy on the *'how are you?'* as it breaks the ice and gets cooperation. Listen to what they say and reply accordingly, but keep it as decently short as possible and without deflecting from the purpose of your call, which is to get paid.

Then get to the point: **'Mary, can you help me please? Our records show you owe \$............ which is now .... weeks overdue.'** Using the person's name and asking for help creates an emotional responsibility for the other party to assist - unless they are professional non-payers, which surprisingly few are.

This, or maybe another call, could be all that is needed to obtain payment, so try and get a firm payment promise by asking, **'Can you pay us today?'** Then wait for their reply. You have now transferred the responsibility to *them* to make a commitment and have kept control.

If they say, **'Yes, we will pay today,'** (some will) thank them for their help and add that you look forward to receiving it tomorrow.

If they say **'We'll do it tomorrow,'** (or next week or sometime) ask for a specific date. **'You will definitely do it tomorrow?'** Pause until you get a commitment and beware of payment promises beyond three days as it means they are buying time. If it is more than three days, squeeze extra information from them to get their help.

'The account is nearly two months old' (sounds worse than saying it is over a month old) **'and we too have bills to pay. Can you pay us now please?'** Adding a bit of drama helps.

A lot of businesses do not like admitting they can't pay, but some are not so shy. The point is to get a firm payment commitment from them. If the person you are speaking to does not have the authority to give that commitment, you have two options.

Either ask them to speak to their boss; '**Will you please ask your accountant** (or other person controlling payments) **for a firm payment date and I will call you back.'** Tell them when you will call (preferably within the hour) to get them to act now and don't forget to phone them …

Or speak to their boss yourself. If the boss is not in, phone again later or get their email address or fax them (see Credit Control by Fax and Email Credit Control chapters).

If by some chance the boss will speak to you, use the above procedures. But you are now talking to a decision-maker, so don't be fobbed off with, **'We will do it next week'**, or worse. Try and get a firm date as you can quote it later if they don't pay. '**Can you give me a date? Will it be Monday?'** Wait for their reply. If they give you a date, thank them and say you will phone on that day to help their memory.

You should know by now if they will pay promptly. If they will not give you a date they may get agitated at being cornered. Keep calm and friendly by implying you know it really won't be necessary to phone back, but you have no choice as it's your job to do so - it's true because if you don't get paid you will run out of money. One of three things then happens:

1. **The Ideal - they pay-up to get rid of you (the squeaky wheel principle).**
2. **They become aggressive or abusive - some believe attack is the best form of defence, so keep calm and say you don't really want to call back** (it's true, you don't). **Tell them they can prevent it by paying - be prepared to negotiate a post-dated cheque provided it is dated no longer than seven days time (post dated cheques are an admission of debt, so they are much better than a promise to transfer the funds), or part payment as long as it begins that week.**
3. **They lie or forget: 'I'll do it today/ tomorrow,' then don't. When that happens - and it does - see next chapter.**

Use the methods in this chapter to train customers to pay promptly. By doing it for several months some, possibly most, will pay on time, or close to it, without being asked. No longer needing to ask for money means your credit control is effective and you will save time and get paid. There might be a hard-core of slow payers and those who enjoy testing their suppliers systems by only paying when asked, plus those who are temporarily short of money, so credit control is still needed. If the reason for late payment is they are not getting paid, buy them a copy of this book. If the reason is more serious, sound credit control reduces exposure and bad debt risk.

The following chapters cover the *what-ifs* and how to overcome them. But if your system is not yet organised, review the previous chapters to put you on the front foot and keep you there.

ACTION PLAN

Are my systems in place?   Yes ☐   No ☐   Partly ☐
If *No* or *Partly*, when will I do it?
_____
_____

My preferred telephone style is (if it differs from ours):
_____
_____
_____
_____

The accounts payable staff I will give thankyou gifts to are:
_____
_____
_____

This is what I will give or do for them:
_____
_____
_____

I will use our Terms of trade to get paid (see *Terms & conditions of trade* chapter)
_____
_____
_____

WHAT IF?

What if the cheque isn't in the mail or there has not been a funds transfer?

Then call, email or fax the debtor. Once again, calling is best because it puts them on the spot if they had promised to pay, so remind them of it. Most people don't like breaking their word, so it can raise you to priority payment status, unless they are a bunch of shysters that is.

What if they have a query or need ... hmm... a copy invoice?

Resolve the query or send a copy invoice – if you run an efficient business disputes are quite rare and they just might genuinely have lost the invoice...

If they feel the dispute is real, they (like you perhaps) are unlikely to pay until you fix it. If you want to sell to them again, fix the problem and think twice about digging your heals in. Ask yourself, *Is it better to keep them as a customer by conceding, or to win and lose their custom?*

If the dispute is just an excuse for not paying, they might now use the 'offence-is-the-best-means-of-defence' tactic, for example *'I told you the other day'* or *'You are hounding me'* or *'I am sick of you b___s phoning me'* and so forth.

ACTION PLAN

Now is a good time to draw up a plan to cope with what if's because it will put you on the front foot instead of the back.

I will handle disputes this way: (for abuse, read next chapter)

_____

_____

_____

_____

_____

_____

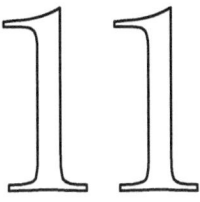

ABUSE

Some people get angry or abusive to justify deceit and professional *I Neverpays* are fond of it. By now you should know there is no genuine dispute. Combat 'the invoice-is-wrong' story by saying, **'You know you are kidding me. Let's work out a payment plan.'**

They may now be honest. Or they may hang up or become more abusive, or still claim they are right. (Ask yourself if they could be.) If they continue abusing you, then try the following.

If it is really getting to you, say, **'I'm ringing off now but I will be back very soon,'** and then hang up.

Alternatively, hold the phone away and don't listen. While you may be tempted to whistle Dixie or something, try not to do so as it is provocative. It can be a good idea to give the impression you are not listening. You are in a stronger position by not listening to abuse because it stops you being drawn into an abuse spiral.

Try and stop them from hanging-up. If the abuse is not getting at you, try and keep them on the line. People don't usually hang up when they are talking or hurling abuse. But hold the phone away as it is best not to listen to ranting. The most likely time they will hang up is when they stop ranting (it is easy to tell, as the noise stops). Because you haven't listened, you are not tempted to answer back as that can make them more abusive.

If they are still on the line, begin with their first name: **'Fred, you know you owe us $_____ (brief pause). You can easily get me off your back without getting angry and spoiling both our days simply by paying.'** Variations can be made to suit the temperament of the person. Humour is an option: **'Fred, you know you are kidding me and you know that I know you are, so how's about making an arrangement to get me off your back?'**

Let them speak next. They now have the problem of deciding whether to pay or to continue holding out, and if they do hold out ask why – they might tell the truth, such as they have no money. If they still deny owing the money, they are either pathological liars or telling the truth. If they do owe it, they may be receptive to paying, or open to a payment plan, so propose one.

If they hang up, or you are forced to, then respond as quickly as possible by fax or email, but a fax is best because it can be seen by other people – see *Credit Control by Fax* chapter. A fax response to verbal abuse is strong stuff. It makes even the most determined non-payer aware the game is up. If you think they may throw then fax in the bin, send it again an hour later or near the end of the day.

If they haven't paid after two days, fax them again because this increases the chance of it being seen by staff, who will see that bills are not paid on time and that increases the odds of you getting paid. If they still don't pay, fax it again and then fax a final demand (see *When to send final demands* chapter). By this stage they should have calmed down unless they really are screwy. If it has got to this stage, you are nearing the end of credit control. The next step could be debt collection as you have done about all you can.

ACTION PLAN – Being prepared for the horrible helps overcome it and relieves stress.

I will handle abuse these ways: (Try and avoid 'If I was a nutcase I'd act just like you.') _____

_____

_____

_____

_____

_____

_____

THE BULLY

Remember the bully at school? Bullies usually capitulate when punched on the nose, and the credit control version of a punch on the nose is threat of legal action, loss of reputation, winding up notices and bad publicity.

The threat of further action in the form of exercising a personal guarantee, bankruptcy, winding up, advising a credit monitoring agency of their non-payment and debt collection may now be justified. If you hesitate without good reason, read chapter 2, *Risk,* again.

Sabre-rattling, which is all you are doing at the moment, is often better than just threatening to close their account. It should have been closed by now to limit your losses, but reminding the bully of that reduces their incentive to pay. They may simply buy from somebody else.

THREATS

The bully's common response to strong action is, 'Are you threatening me?' This is a superb way to get you off their back, as suddenly you are being accused of nasty behaviour and it is easy to forget that you are in the right.

Respond by calling their bluff. If they say, **'Are you threatening me?'** respond with, **'Yes, I sincerely hope so,'** or **'I'm just telling you what will happen,'** (i.e. either winding up or debt collection), or **'You can stop it by paying now.'**

If you remain calm the bully will run out of steam and then you can strike back with a calculated response, such as; **'You have 24 hours to pay and if you don't this is what's going to happen.'** Because they owe you money you have a number of ultimatum options, so spell them out. You might have thought of some while they were ranting, but having a list of prepared responses is more effective because you can reel them off one by one in an impressive way. The rest of this book will give you ideas on what your remedies are, so list them in your Action Plan box to give the bully a broadside

If you have done credit checks on potential credit account customers before granting credit you can identify bullies in advance and decide whether to sell to them on credit or not. It might be better to offer the bullyboys and girls a cash discount instead if you really want their business because, as in schools, there are also bullies in business. They probably do not bully their customers, otherwise they would be out of business, but suppliers are fair game.

ACTION PLAN – if you've been bullied you probably know how to overcome it. If you were a bully, it's repentance time.

This is how I will handle bullies _____

_____

_____

_____

These are my ultimatum options _____

_____

_____

_____

13

MESSRS. I NEVERPAY

Professional *I Neverpays'* are usually not bullies. They are more subtle and can have no intention of paying, or failing that, delay it as long as possible

One talented but time-wasting *I Neverpay* only owed $600 and apart from asking for copy invoices, did not dispute the debt. Payment had been in the mail for over a year and when it wasn't in the mail the response was simply, 'We *don't have the money.'*

All credit control methods had been used and letters from a debt collector sent. That didn't work either because the debtor knew how to handle them. The response was, 'We don't care - take us to the Small Claims Court, any court, Hampton Court, because we can only pay $1 a week.' This debtor never intended to pay and knew it was unlikely that anyone would sue for $600 as the result would not be worth it because I Neverpay traded as a company and calmly said they would liquidate it if they were sued.

The debtor was always polite and never abusive. She had lots of time to say how bad things were in her industry (a sympathy request) and said she was not going to pay because she had bad debts too.

The supplier closed the account at 60 days, limiting their exposure to a manageable $600. As not every story has a happy ending, try and limit your exposure if you meet a real *I Neverpay.*

If their terms of trade had been up-to-date they would have been able to collect the debt, plus all recovery costs and interest, so recovery action would have been worth it. But at that time they did not, and they might have been faced with a bill higher than the debt. If they had obtained personal guarantees, Ms I Neverpay would probably have paid on receipt of the following *Recovery Action: Final Notice* fax. The lost $600 was all the stimulus needed to get fully enforceable terms of trade signed by debtors and to do credit checks before opening new accounts. (Do you have enforceable terms of trade and do credit checks?). If purchases are likely to be more than $5,000 a month and if new customers are companies, they now insist on personal guarantees. They tried to get guarantees on monthly purchases of $2,000, but as nobody else in their industry did this, they dropped the idea. Sometimes you have to accept modest risks as a cost of doing business and in normal times in most industries, bad debt risk is controllable. But in addition to credit checks on new customers, they also do them on existing ones when purchases increase substantially and if a bad debt would harm them.

Another *I Neverpay* I know is a retailer who is expert at fobbing-off suppliers, many of whom are small manufacturers or wholesalers. *Roger the Dodger's* shop is high-profile in a quality mall and retails up-market products. It is a sophisticated business run by a person with commercial acumen who is skilled in his trade and the art of delaying payment.

Fortunately, one of their suppliers has good terms of trade and insists on personal guarantees from customers who operate as limited liability companies and others who could wriggle out of paying their debts. The following sabre-rattling fax to Roger obtained 50% payment by return and the balance was paid two weeks later. Roger still buys from the supplier and often tries to pay late (to test the waters) but one call usually brings him into line.

It took a while for the client to agree to the following fax being sent. Prior to this they had closed the account, which stopped further exposure, but reduced the debtor's incentive to pay as he could get similar products elsewhere.

The Good Service Company Ltd
123 Busy Street, Industryville

Date _____

Mr. I. Neverpay,
I Neverpay Specialists,
100 Debt Street,
Debtorsville

Mr. Neverpay,

RECOVERY ACTION: FINAL NOTICE

Despite previous payment requests which you have ignored, we are now obliged to take recovery action for the sum of $_____ owed by you.

This is now a **FINAL NOTICE** for immediate payment. To prevent action being taken against you without further notice please pay us today.

Yours faithfully,

Credit Controller

Our first action will be to call upon the Personal Guarantee you signed. This makes you personally liable for the above debts plus all other costs and amounts owing, including cost of recovery and legal fees. Failure to pay could result in your bankruptcy or other proceedings against you.'

Immediate payment will prevent this.

(The above is referred to as Remind 3 elsewhere in this book)

Action Plan – it's fun and profitable knowing how to overcome poor payers.

I will handle *I Neverpay's* this way _____

_____

_____

_____

_____

_____

_____

14

IMPORTANCE OF WRITTEN NOTES

A client was owed $8,200 by a restaurant that was up for sale. After hearing a sob story from the restaurateur, the client agreed to accept payment after the restaurant was sold.

We were asked by the creditor to keep reminding the restaurateur of his obligations but not to get tough. *'You will be paid in full as soon as the sale goes through,'* was his reassurance.

We recorded all his payment promises, including the dates and times they were made. The restaurant was eventually sold, but instead of receiving $8,200, a cheque for $7000 came instead along with a letter from his lawyer. The letter stated that the $7,000 was in full and final settlement and that by banking the cheque it meant that the full and final settlement offer had been accepted. We suggested to the client that he phone his lawyer, who told him that a bird in the hand was worth two in the bush, so bank the cheque then immediately write to the debtor saying it had been banked as a part payment and not as full and final settlement.

It turned out that almost all the restaurateur's other creditors had accepted part payment as full and final without asking if it was legally binding. We do not know if the lawyer was given a free lunch in exchange for writing the letter, but even if the restaurateur had to pay the lawyer he still saved around $30,000.

Our client had a personal guarantee and we had notes of all conversations, including the dates and times. When the former restaurateur was reminded of this he paid the $1,200 shortfall. If notes had not existed it would have been a different story and the shortfall might never have been paid without a fight, so keep a record of all promises including the names of the people who made them and the dates and times. If you have accounts software with a credit control module, or customer relationship management software (CRM), use it instead of bits of paper which can get lost. Good software makes credit control quicker and more effective, but remember to do regular back-ups.

ACTION PLAN

This is where I will keep written notes:
Computer and/or CRM software ☐
Note Book ☐
Other ☐ If other, where? _____

I will make notes during or immediately after contacting the debtor Yes ☐

BLOCKERS

Blocking is more frequent in larger companies because smaller firms lack the staff to do it successfully.

It won't take long to discover you are being blocked, but time is often in short supply, so you could be tempted to hang up. Blockers know this, but unless you breach the block you will not get paid until they feel like paying, so don't quit. Sure, you have other things to do, but getting paid is fundamental because without it you will not be in business for long, so stick at it.

Blocking is another reason why effective terms and conditions of trade are needed because they give you ammunition to persuade slow payers to pay, such as high rates of interest, which adds to their costs. Set the interest at credit card rates, or higher, as credit card rates provide a benchmark which makes it harder for you to be accused of usury, even though it is exorbitant. If you have a clause allowing for penalty interest on overdue accounts in your terms of trade, make out the interest invoice while they keep you waiting - you will then be using the time to increase revenue.

Operators who ask, *'May I say who is calling?'* and when you tell them say, *'I'm sorry they are in a meeting,'* could be blocking you. They certainly are if similar stories are told every time.

Skilful blockers can fob you off for days, or weeks, if you let them. *'I'm sorry they are not in* (they have the flu/bubonic plague) *but I'll give them your message.'* Usually, there is nobody else who can help you - they all have the plague, so you are given the run-around.

Caller ID adds to their armoury, so if you suspect they are identifying you before answering the phone, prefix your call with a number block and if you don't know the prefix, ask your phone company.

Ways to overcome blocking are to keep the operator on the phone for as long as possible whilst making out the interest invoice. Ask questions such as, **'When will the meeting end? When are they likely to be back?'** This means the blocker cannot do their job while talking to you. After a minute or so they will show anxiety signs - they can't wait to get rid of you. Before they hang up say, **'I know you are doing your job, and doing it well, but you know you are fobbing me off** (short pause). **You've done your best, so kindly put me through right now.'**

This works if the operator is blocking - they'll soon tell you if they are not.

While faxes or emails usually get through if they are genuinely in a meeting, professional non-payers bin or delete them. But faxes have a distinct advantage as shown in the *Credit control by fax* chapter.

In addition to the phone, ways to overcome blocking are:

Emails - start with one email on the first day, send two next day (one in the morning and one after lunch) and three on day three. Care should be taken not to send more than three a day because they will probably put you on their block sender list if they have not already done so. After four days, refer to the *When to send final demands* chapter.

Faxes – send one on day one, two the next day and three on day three. It is hard to block a fax, so they are almost always received. Unlike emails, faxes are often seen by other staff and it is easy to send final demand faxes too, which can also be seen by employees, so faxes are effective anti-blocking tools.

The above are usual anti-blocking options - if you have others write them here:

My anti-blocking options are:

_____

_____

_____

_____

AN EVERYDAY STORY OF BLOCKING FOLK

These blocking folk inhabit a company operating from up-market premises and the directors have cars to match.

Creditors provide their working capital as they pay at 120 days, or later if they can get away with it.

They are master blockers and could write a book on it. But they are vulnerable to the keep-their-operator-talking anti-blocking method. They change operators frequently, probably for fatigue reasons, as staff can find telling lies stressful after a while.

Getting through the *they-are-in-a-meeting* block only breaches their first defence. The second is their accounts payable department, who are programmed to say, 'the *payment run has been done and is awaiting our financial controller's authorisation'*. Trouble is the poor guy is always in meetings/away/has the plague. When you finally get through to the financial controller, the comment is, '*I will sign it now. The cheque will be in the mail tonight*' or tomorrow or payment will be direct credited. This is a very slick *I Neverpay* operation from a company that usually gets away with paying late.

The only way of getting paid sooner is to speak to their CEO - when he's in, that is. As a variation to the *in-a-meeting,* or *got-the-flu* theme, their CEO is a globe trotter. He did, though, once give an e-mail assurance of prompt payment. This is cherished. It is worth far more than its weight in gold and is regularly emailed and faxed back to him (in case he has put us on his blocked senders list) as a reminder of his promise. When that doesn't work he is phoned on his direct line or mobile, prefixed by the delete caller ID number because he seems to knows the names of dozens of credit staff by heart and ignores their calls. His direct line and mobile numbers were obtained by asking the person who places the orders and saying we wanted to arrange a little something for his boss. Saying we wanted to arrange something was true, but not the little something they thought it was.

It is a shame to have to use subterfuge, but if faced with a determined *I Neverpay*, you may need to. Persistence gets this account paid, but has to be repeated every second or third month because they have short memories and are resistant to being trained to pay promptly.

Other suppliers seem to accept late payment - they must do, as they keep selling to them. But persistence wins and as Sir Winston Churchill said, *'Never give in, never give in, never give in...'*

This company, a high-profile purveyor of quality goods, shamelessly uses creditors money to finance its business. They have a financial controller and layers of support management, but they are a default risk. Sophisticated companies go bust, often spectacularly. Our client gets paid at around 45 days instead of the debtor's preferred 90 to 120 day (or longer) payment times, but if the company defaulted, some creditors would incur bad debts of three to four months sales. Would you survive such a loss?

Keep notes of promises made by companies like this. Record promises, names, dates and time of conversations - it could be useful evidence later and be accepted as a personal liability to pay you. The e-mail from their CEO may not be evidence of personal liability, but is useful for getting paid. Work out what levers you can use to get money out of the business equivalent of stones.

ACTION PLAN

My tactics and levers with blockers & 'Neverpays' will be _____

_____

_____

_____

_____

_____

16

ACCOUNT RECONCILIATION EXCUSE

Ensuring invoices are correct before paying them is reasonable, but some businesses have extraordinary difficulties with reconciliation or lost invoices.

Often it is just another excuse to delay payment. One of the companies in the previous chapter staples two invoices together in the belief they are one, then claims the unpaid invoice has been paid. With the creditor's approval, we told their accounts payable clerk and financial controller that their systems were deficient. As few people enjoy being regarded as bunnies, the system improved a bit. Most businesses are not this shameless and if you come across one there is little risk of damage to customer relations if you do likewise as accounts staff rarely make the buying decisions.

In practice, it is usually more substantial businesses that use blocking and account reconciliation excuses. Small ones do not have the staff and are usually more straightforward to deal with. Instead, they generally tell you it's in the next payment run; the cheque's-in-the-mail; or that they need a copy invoice; or they can't pay you until a big customer pays them; or say they thought they had paid already and so on.

Debtors on seven-day accounts can have real reconciliation problems, especially when some purchases are payment at seven days and others at month-end. Month-end statements are needed to help debtors reconcile their account in these cases. As seven-day accounts can be subject to special prices, or prompt-payment discounts, they will be tempted to pay late if the deadline is missed. Sound credit control skills are then needed to coax them back into line, but avoid offering to grant the discount or special prices provided they pay today more than once. Repeating it will result in your payment-in-seven-days incentive being blown to bits.

ACTION PLAN

My reconciliation problem plan is _____

_____

_____

_____

_____

_____

THE CHEQUE'S IN THE MAIL

Cheques (*checks* in US) are falling out of fashion, but they are proof of debt so are very valuable as mentioned in the *Selecting your credit controller* chapter. Try and get a cheque if there is a possibility of the debtor disputing the debt later. If you still pay by cheque, don't stop issuing them just to gain a non-payment excuse as that would be dishonest.

The cheque's in the mail excuse has been overused and has lost most of its credibility even when it is true, which it rarely is. While most of us have experienced delays, these are mainly caused by the sender inadequately addressing the envelope – in the case of cheques it can be deliberate.

Exotic variations to lost-in-the-mail have been used, such as, '*the mail box was destroyed by a truck after I posted your cheque. As you haven't got it, this must have happened before it was emptied. I will have to cancel it, but am busy so can't go to the bank or wait until their call centre answers the phone.*' This story bought this debtor an extra two weeks and whether the tale was true or not, it worked! Fortunately, internet banking has effectively eliminated *your bank must have lost the deposit* story. For such yarns to be plausible there has to be an external party to blame, preferably one that cannot easily be approached to check its validity.

Sometimes the cheque may be in the mail. But for slow payers, *The cheque's in the mail* means:

> **'Get off my back and go away.'**
> **'It will be in the mail now you've asked me again.'**
> **'We didn't mail it because ...'**
> **'On my one-to-ten list of priorities, paying you ranks as minus three.'**

and anything else they can think of.
Ways to handle this are to ask:

> **When was it mailed?**
> **What was the amount?**
> **Has the cheque been presented to your bank?**

Some of these are also questions to ask those who have really paid their account. However, it puts bluffers under pressure as they have to lie, own up or pay straightaway in order to cover up.

If you suspect they are kidding, say, **'I'm not sure what the mail is coming to as you are the sixth person who has told me that.'** A short pause increases the drama.

Next say, **'Shall we leave it for a day? If it doesn't arrive by tomorrow, I will phone you. As you mailed it when you said, it's bound to be here by then.'** This gives them a chance to save face by actually sending it.

ACTION PLAN

My preferred style is _____

_____

_____

_____

_____

_____

DIRECT CREDITS

Paying by direct credit (internet banking, EFT or similar) is standard practice for most businesses, some of which no longer use cheques, or only do so under unusual circumstances. But internet banking gives *I Neverpays'* even better excuses than 'the cheque's in the mail.'

You can tell if a cheque has arrived by simply waiting for the mail. No effort is needed as it is either there or it is not.

Effort is needed to see if a direct credit has been made. Instead of just waiting for the mail, you have to check your bank account to see if it has happened. This takes time even with internet banking and other work pressures can delay it and then it can be overlooked. You also need internet access and if you are busy, or someone else is on your/the only computer (common in small businesses) it is frustrating. It takes longer if you have to use telephone banking, or physically go to the bank and get a mini-statement, or wait until you next receive a bank statement, perhaps at month-end.

While bigger outfits have the staff to monitor their bank account, small ones often do not. If yours is a small business, you may not have time to check your bank account regularly. But comments from debtors such as, 'We *will direct credit you today'* and then not doing so are frequent.

Apart from checking your bank account regularly, there is no quick-fix solution. Once you discover a debtor has misled you with the, *'we-will-do-it-today'* story then, unless it is a genuine omission, regard them with the same suspicion you would with *the cheque's-in-the-mail* types and use similar methods when calling them, such as:

> **Has it been charged to your account? If it has, it could be fraud so you must contact the police because it isn't in our account.** Then pause to gauge their reaction ...

> If they still claim they have done it and it is not shown on their bank account say:

> **When did you do the transfer?**
> **What was the amount?**
> **What account did you send it to?**

> If you still suspect they are kidding, say, **'The banking system must be collapsing as you are the fourth person who has told me that.'** After a short pause say, **'Shall we leave it for a day? If it isn't in our account by tomorrow, I will phone you.** This gives them a chance to save face by actually doing it.

If they go through the same rigmarole in future and you cannot check your account regularly, say something like, **'Please email or fax the payment receipt from your bank for my records as soon as you do it.'** While this is not ideal, it is the best option at the moment.

The other issue with bank transfers is the risk that the creditor enters the wrong account details and either sends it to somebody else, or it is an invalid account number, because either way you will not get paid. If they have sent it to the wrong account, especially if it is to another person or business, they could say they cannot pay until they get their money back. That could take time, or might not happen at all. Unless you gave them wrong account details this is not your problem, so refuse to accept any further delays because it was their mistake and not yours. Then get tough if they don't pay promptly.

ACTION PLAN

My direct credit tactics are _____

_____

_____

_____

_____

_____

_____

19

CREDIT CONTROL BY FAX

Faxes are great credit control tools and are much better than letters because they are received immediately. They can be much better than emails too because unlike emails they can easily be seen by other people. If you cannot send or receive faxes by computer, or other device, buy a cheap fax machine or do a web search by entering *fax solutions, faxability, faxmate* or similar to find a fax subscription service.

If you are one of the increasing number of people who no longer have copper wire landlines, your mobile or other device (shop around as any options written here will be obsolete tomorrow) could be used to send faxes and perhaps receive them. If you have a landline, there could be a fax option enabling a fax and phone to operate on one line but not every phone company has this. If you already have two numbers on one line, such as your home and a business number, it may be hard to have a fax option as well. If so, a solution (less than ideal but a quick-fix) is allocating one of the numbers for the fax and only plugging the fax in when sending one, or when the fax tone is heard on an incoming call. Don't worry if you fail to plug the fax in quickly enough because the sender's fax should automatically send it again a few minutes later (most do it three times before giving up). If these options do not work, or it is too hard, either an extra line could be needed, or forget the copper wire completely and acquire a mobile-type solution.

Some days you just don't feel like phoning and a fax is an effective way of getting paid. It gets the job done without verbal fencing and, like emails, faxes can be sent out of working hours. Other fax advantages that emails do not have are:

- **If the person who pays the bills is away a fax is likely to be seen by other people whilst emails are not.**

- **The fax is less aggressive and avoids confrontations with slow payers**. This is useful for the 'cheque's-in-the-mail' types if the promised cheque is not in the mail. A handwritten comment saying, *you promised to pay on* (date), *please keep your word!* works well. It can be faxed again with extra handwritten comments again to be seen by others in the business.

The following sample faxes can be used:

FAX 1

This is a polite reminder. The name and address can be handwritten to save time and can be sent more than once by changing the date, which reminds the debtor it has been sent before. If you are sending faxes by computer or CRM then create a template.

The Good Service Company Limited
123 Busy Street, Industryville

(Date)

Mr. Iwill Neverpay,
I Neverpay Specialists.

Dear Iwill,

Your account is now overdue.

If you have paid the $_____ you owe us, then we apologise. However, if it has been overlooked please, pay us **today,** or urgently phone us if you are dissatisfied with the service we have given you.

Thank you for helping us to help you grow your business.

Yours sincerely,
Good Service Company Ltd,

Credit Controller

FAX 2

This is stronger and used when either phone calls have not worked or Fax 1 has been ignored. It can also be sent more than once by changing the date and adding extra comments - if sending them manually, handwritten comments are best because they are eye-catching and are more likely to be acted on.

The Good Service Company Limited
123 Busy Street, Industryville

(Date)
Mr. I. Neverpay,
I Neverpay Specialists.

Dear Mr Neverpay

After previously asking you, we trusted it wasn't necessary to ask again about your **Unpaid Account.**

We must now request you to **honour our payment terms**, which have been **exceeded**. If your payment of $_____ has already been sent, then we apologise. If it has been overlooked, then to maintain your credit worthiness please send it immediately.

Yours sincerely,
Good Service Company Ltd,

Credit Controller

Faxes reduce confrontation risk and as they can be seen by junior staff who discover that bills are not being paid, it helps to deter managers from ignoring them as further ones may follow, to be seen again by staff. This is non-aggressive embarrassment that rarely impacts on the relationship between you and the customer. It certainly speeds up payment.

If your CRM or accounts software has a credit control module, you can send faxes automatically. Whilst they won't be as personalised, they can work and save time. If they do not work, send them manually with handwritten comments.

When sending faxes manually, handwriting the debtor's name on the fax with *Dear (first name)* is more effective than typing it. There are so many computer-generated personal letters that a typed name is no longer personal. Handwriting the person's name on the fax shows you are taking the time to write personally. When you sign your name, just put your first name and write it so the reader can decipher it.

If you have to re-send the fax, handwrite the new date and add a few extra comments to remind them it is not the first time you have asked: '*You promised to pay us on* (date). *Please honour your commitment.*' This puts the obligation onto the recipient who had previously said they would pay.

In the *When to send final demands* chapter there is a final demand fax. Faxing a final demand is effective because it can be seen by staff and even if it is not, it has an impact. When final demands are faxed they rarely need to be mailed as payment has either occurred, or an arrangement put in place before the demand's expiry date.

ACTION PLAN

I will send faxes during working hours   Yes ☐ Sometimes ☐

If Yes or Sometimes when? (times and dates) _____

_____

I will send faxes after hours   Yes ☐ Sometimes ☐

If Yes or Sometimes, when (times and dates) _____

_____

I will/can use my computer   Yes ☐ Sometimes ☐

I will use our fax machine   Yes ☐ Sometimes ☐

I will use an online fax service   Yes ☐ Sometimes ☐

I will use/modify the faxes in this book   Yes ☐ No ☐ If No

what will I do? _____

Other options are _____

_____

EMAIL CREDIT CONTROL

Unlike faxes, emails are often only seen by the recipient so they fail to create the non-aggressive discomfort of staff learning that the business doesn't pay its bills.

Sending credit control emails to the person who places the orders may not be a good idea because they are your customer, so they need to be sent to the accounts payable person. Their email address is needed and might be hard, or time consuming, to get or they may not have one. An increasing number of outfits are restricting internet and email usage because of unnecessary correspondence and abuse, such as private affairs or browsing when they should be working.

Emails are also easy to delete. They may be deleted before being read, or if they are read, a click sends them into oblivion. On the other hand, frequent reminders are easy if you know the accounts payable person's email address, and probably their accountant's or financial controller's too. If things get really bad, you can always email the boss. Phoning could be more diplomatic and successful, so work out which is the best thing to do.

If you want a subject heading, consider using 'Unpaid Account'. But if the debtor is a professional *I. Neverpay*, they could delete it unread if their procedure is to get rid of things they don't like. But if you are sending a closure of account notice, or a final demand, use that as the subject because they are more likely to read stuff like that.

The following is an email to adapt to suit the circumstances and if payment doesn't come, adapt the faxes in the previous chapter.

(insert recipients e-mail address)

Dear _____

Your account is now overdue and you owe us $_____

Please pay us now or contact me if payment will be delayed for any reason.

Yours sincerely,

(your name)

(your company name)

ACTION PLAN

Can I easily send credit control emails to all my debtors?   Yes ☐ No ☐

Can I easily send credit control emails to my major debtors? Yes ☐ No ☐

If *No* this is how I can get their email addresses? _____

_____

_____

I will get their email addresses by (date) _____

_____

21

NEVER GIVE IN, NEVER, NEVER, NEVER...

During the darker days of World War 2, Winston Churchill gave a speech at his old school, Harrow, in North London and began with: 'Never give in, never give in, never, never, never, never: in nothing great or small, large or petty – never give in – except to convictions of honour and good sense.'

Don't quit applies to many aspects of life, and to credit control. If you persevere you can succeed. If you quit you probably won't. So don't snatch defeat from the jaws of victory by giving up just because something you have tried isn't working. If we all knew what works all the time and what doesn't work, then everything would always work, wouldn't it?

Don't quit - those who do just join the queue, so keep at it because as the following example shows repetition often wins in the end

Success through repetition
(Debtors less than 60 days overdue)

Success through repetition (Debtors under 60- days overdue)	
Number of contacts with the Debtor	**Payment Success % in a buoyant economy**
1st. time	32%
2nd. Time	55%
3rd. time	72%
4th. Time	88%
5th. Time	94%

Source: Accounts Receivable Solutions

When the economy is buoyant and money is not in short supply, after 3 contacts 72% of overdue debtors will have paid, so you will not need to contact them again that month. Even in good times some customers will be short of money because that's the way business is, so prompt them to make yours a priority payment by frequently contacting them. Judgement is required on how to handle customers who are going through a tough patch, but success in business depends on sound judgements. When money is tight, such as in a mild recession, the payment success rate drops and one to two extra contacts are needed. When a recession worsens, three or more extra contacts could be necessary and if things worsen and a depression occurs, overall business strategy needs revising, especially credit policy.

The *Success through repetition* statistics only applies to debtors less than 60 days overdue. If they reach 90 days, or beyond, you are faced with a hardcore of poor payers. If it gets to that, refer to the *When to send final demands* chapter unless the reason is caused by an issue that is your problem and remains unfixed, such as a product defect and you are awaiting replacement parts. This issue might not be your fault, but it is your problem and not theirs and they are unlikely to pay until it is fixed – you might do likewise if you were the customer.

Prepare your never-give-in plans for front-foot solutions when things get tough. If a reason for delayed payment could be caused by product or other defects, or is your suppliers fault, figure out how to overcome them. This can provide solutions when customers say, *'we are not paying because ….'* Solutions could include making an agreement with suppliers to defer payment for their lack of inventory or faulty goods you are on-selling and other solutions applicable to your business.

ACTION PLAN

My never-give-in solutions are _____

_____

_____

_____

Issues that could stop customers from paying are _____

_____

_____

_____

Solutions are _____

_____

_____

_____

'**I CAN'T PAY YOU UNTIL THEY PAY ME'**

'*I* can't pay you until they pay me,' is another favourite 'we-can't-pay' excuse that debtors use effectively to get creditors off their backs. It works because it can be true.

Debtors sometimes say they cannot pay until they are paid to get your sympathy - they may really need it too - but it deflects from your objective of getting paid. Your aim is to get people who say, '*I can't pay you until they pay me*' to upgrade you to a priority creditor and to pay you before paying anyone else.

Contact them regularly, or offer to help them get paid. It is unlikely they will let you do this, especially if '*I cannot pay you until they pay me*' is simply an excuse. If it is, they may think about paying to shut you up.

If they truly cannot pay you until they are paid, suggest they buy a copy of this book. As they are your customer, give them one because by helping them you will be helping yourself.

Ways of combating 'I can't pay you until they pay me' are:

1. **What are you doing to get paid?**
2. **Can I contact your customer for you?**
3. **Do you have an overdraft facility?**
4. **Can you give us a post dated cheque?**
   Cheques post-dated more than a week need careful consideration, but it does effectively stop them from disputing the debt later.
5. **Say, 'When you bought from us you never said you couldn't pay. Our terms are payment on (date) of the month. What commitment can you now make?'**

Unless you have the time and expertise, there is probably little you can do to help a customer to get paid. But you might be able to help them some other way without risking a bad debt or spending too much time. They are your customer and you probably want them to buy from you again, so if you can help them overcome a temporary problem, they could increase their spend or remain loyal. How to help them depends on their, and your, circumstances and could include:

* **Not closing their account** (unless it is a large amount that is long overdue and they are likely to go broke).
* **Continuing supply on a cash sale basis.**
* **Accepting part payments** (make the first one this week if possible).
* **Arrange a contra** (if you owe them money, credit their account with what they owe you and get them to do likewise. In case they go broke, get them to agree to

the contra in writing – an email could do – as that might help prevent a claw-back by a receiver).

- **Swap** (buy some of their goods/services and credit their account with the cost).
- **Free service** (they do something free and you credit their account with the value of it – if they are a garage, a free service (or labour free) or free labour to paint your premises).
- **Other** – as applicable to your and their business

Action Plan – write down your options to be prepared for when it happens.

My 'I can't pay you' plan is:
Buy them this book ☐
Other solutions ☐ **which are:** _____

_____
_____
_____
_____
_____

WHEN TO SEND FINAL DEMANDS

Sending final demands is the end of credit control and the start of debt collection. To save money, you can send your own final demand letter by copying the one in this chapter, or hand it over to a lawyer or a debt collector.

The time to push the *blast 'em* button is when credit control has failed, or when payment promises have been broken, or if they are about to go broke and there is nothing you can do to help them. Also press it when *I can't pay* becomes *I won't pay* and when they have refused to accept a reasonable compromise to a dispute. Reasonable though means *reasonable* not just to you, but to them as well and is what an impartial outsider (and a court) would class as *reasonable*. Sometimes, accepting a reasonable compromise can obtain payment, save legal costs (and risk of losing the case and having to pay their costs) plus keep them as a customer.

If you send a final demand requiring payment within seven days, contact them three days after sending it for a final verbal attempt to get paid. Then take recovery action immediately after the payment notice expires.

If they cannot pay immediately and you do not want to hand them over, seek legal advice. Obtaining a signed letter of intent to pay from a director or shareholder to personally pay helps. Insist on them doing this immediately - if they are confident in their company, then they can put their personal assets where their company mouth is. Also, ask for a rigid payment plan starting ASAP with the final payment within a time acceptable to you. This should start this week and not next month, otherwise they are getting you off their backs and you are not getting your money.

The above can be better than resorting to debt collection. While it may stretch your relations with them, it might not destroy them. If the debtor is going through a temporary rough time, perhaps caused by them suffering a bad debt, easing up slightly (but not giving in and doing nothing) may keep them as a customer for years.

Have your lawyer tie everything up, including any possible dispute issues and other grey areas, or if a receiver or other party attempts to recover money paid to you by the debtor. This happens if the receiver or liquidator believes you have jumped the payment queue and is known as **voidable preference** (see *Legal stuff* chapter). Great care is needed to overcome a voidable preference claim made against you, which is likely to be made by a receiver, or other member of the sour grape crowd, who want to relieve you of your own money. They can often to do this for payments made by the creditor six months ago, and in some instances and jurisdictions, for payments made even earlier. A court judgment can force you to repay what is your money under a range of circumstances, including getting paid before other creditors. This penalizes you for being businesslike and seems seem unjust, but sometimes it appears that the law has little to do with justice. So, should you suspect this could happen, urgently seek legal advice. Say or write nothing until you have got it.

In practice, if you get paid before they go broke, possession by you of your own money can be nine tenths of the law. If the amount is not high and you make it hard for them, receivers sometimes do not bother to take matters further. A priority receivers and the like have is to ensure that the organisation which engaged them (a debenture holder, such as a bank) gets as much money back as possible. That means preferably all of it, provided the cost of recovery does not exceed the amount recovered. If you can show that in your case they will not achieve it, they usually go away if the amount is smallish.

If you have been dealing with a bunch of shysters, hand them over. The expression *shyster* probably comes from a 19th century New York lawyer called Scheuster. A 1920s shyster was Charles Ponzi, and Ponzi is now the name of a type of fraud. But if your customer is just suffering a temporary setback, handing them over can cause them to go broke, or to dig their heels in and turn them from a willing, *'I can't pay just yet,'* to a, *'I'm not going to pay for as long as possible, regardless of whether I can or not.'*

If you do not have a personal guarantee, or a personal letter of intent to pay, and feel they are about to collapse, act quickly. Ask them how much they owe other creditors, and how close they are to going bust. This is where legal advice is vital so you can get paid before the dogs go in, and then keep your money after they do.

The following is an example of a final demand (known in the trade as a *dunning letter*) to send or modify. Try faxing it to increase the chances of staff seeing it because if they do the money could be in your bank the next day. Mail it if they don't pay within 24 hours and it should be the last letter you send, as after this it becomes debt collection.

PRIVATE AND CONFIDENTIAL

(Date)

Mr. I. Neverpay,
Neverpay Specialists,
P. O. Box 100,
Debtorsville.

Mr Neverpay,

Without Prejudice

Despite repeated requests you have not paid the $_____ you owe us.

Be advised that ownership of all goods supplied to you remains with us. Our remedies to recover your debt include the immediate repossession of goods supplied by us in accordance with our terms and condition of trade without further reference to you. This could damage your business. Other remedies include, but are not necessarily limited to, court action.

A credit rating report on you is now being sought from a credit surveillance and recovery specialist. Such reports show details of assets, liabilities, court actions, bankruptcy, other matters or sums owed to secured and unsecured creditors. This report will be supplied to other businesses you owe money to without further reference to you.

By immediately paying us you will avoid both the above and debt collection which will start within three days, **or Sooner** if the credit report gives us concern about your ability to pay. Such action will be without further notice to you.

By immediately paying us you will avoid the above actions. Such action will be without further notice to you.

Yours faithfully,

Credit Controller
Note: Immediate payment will save you from this

A dunning letter

If you are reluctant to get tough with delinquents, read the *Risk* chapter again. If they are a friend or relative, remind them that good friends and relatives do not let each other down. If they really are decent and worthwhile knowing, insist they pay you right now.

Action Plan - delay is a thief of money. There may not be a warning of collapse and being prepared increases the odds of getting paid.

<u>**My final demand action plan is:**</u>

☐ Contact my lawyer - name and phone numbers are ___

_____

Hand them over to:

☐ Lawyer (name and number if different to above) _____

_____

☐ Debt collector if I do not want my lawyer (name and number) _____

_____

☐ Other plans/contingenci _____

_____

_____

_____

_____

LAST STAND

If you won't start recovery action for whatever reasons, (sound reasons and not excuses for dithering) try a last attempt to get paid. But first jot down your action plan in case it fails – to stimulate you, jot down the consequences if it does ...

Last stands include refusing to release partially completed work and withholding documentation, artwork, moulds or anything else belonging to the debtor which is in your possession. But first check the retention of title clauses on your terms of trade - see *Terms & conditions of trade* chapter – or call your lawyer if in doubt, or if there could be problems. These could arise if you have to enter their premises, or the items you possess belong to a third party, such as equipment sent to you for subcontract work.

Knowing your strengths and weaknesses saves time, complications and money by putting you on the front foot if the horrible happens. Also, find out what to do if the debtor or a receiver threatens you, or they or a repossession agent calls to collect goods in your possession. It's thrilling, and fun, knowing how to send such folk packing and it puts you in a much stronger position to get your money.

Possession can be nine tenths of the law and withholding materials, especially if they are crucial to the debtor's or receiver's interests, results in payment, or the best outcome in a bad situation, by standing your ground. They will huff and puff but if you are within your rights, so what! Even receivers have been known to pay an unsecured creditor to ensure the secured creditor receives a greater pay-out, or to maintain the going concern value of a business. But never seize anybody else's property in your possession without knowing your rights and responsibilities. If you go to their premises to collect materials you have supplied, legal advice is vital beforehand. **It could save you from criminal charges.**

If it gets to this stage, credit control has ended. Recovery, or bad debt, is next.

Action Plan – fill it in now to increases the odds of getting your money.

Last Stand plans are _____
_____
_____

If I don't get paid, consequences are _____
_____
_____

If they let me down, this is what I will/can do
_____
_____

BOUNCED CHEQUES

It takes days for cheques to clear, so you might not know it has bounced for up to a week. If you have doubts, ask your bank to see if they can do a same-day clearance and although there is a charge, it can be worth it.

Once upon a time, banks used to return the original cheque with a note saying, *present again, insufficient funds, refer to drawer* or *payment stopped*. Few banks now return the original cheque and the only comment they make is 'payment stopped' or 'refer to drawer' *Payment stopped* means they have changed their minds about paying you, which could mean they are going to dispute the debt. *Refer to drawer* means that there is no point in redepositing the cheque because it will not be honoured, so you have to contact your customer and obtain payment by other means, such as cash or credit card.

Although the drawer is charged a fee for issuing a dud cheque, this is little comfort. But, as mentioned earlier, the cheque can be evidence they owe you the money, so contact your bank and ask for a copy. The original might not be available as many banks now destroy cheques after a week or so, but they are/should be scanned first, so they can provide a copy – get them to legally certify it in case it goes to court as they should be used to doing this.

If the drawer says, *'It was a mistake and it should never have bounced, so deposit it again,'* and if you don't have the original you will have to get your bank to present (deposit) it again for you. It will then take time before you know if it has been honoured or bounces again. If it does or the drawer says, *'I have no money,'* then what do you do?

Assuming that you know how to contact your customer (if you don't, you have just incurred a bad debt) your options are:

- **Repossess your goods.**
- **Withhold property in your possession.**
- **Visit them and ask for cash, and stay until you get it.**
- **See your lawyer, especially if the amount is large, or hand them over to a debt collector.**

Action Plan. If they can't pay you they probably can't pay the others, so do it now.

My bounced cheque action plan is _____

_____

_____

_____

_____

_____

DEBT COLLECTION

Debt collection just might be a management failure.
It is also a profitable business to be in ...

Unless the debtor unreasonably refuses to pay or has been deceptive, fraudulent or the victim of something similar, resorting to debt collection is a management failure. If systems had been in place and adhered to, plus credit checks done – including checks on existing customers who owe heaps and those who might be shaky - the need for debt collection could almost be eliminated.

Whilst poor credit management is a main reason for B2B debt collection, it can be brought about by disputes or similar problems. If these cannot be fixed in a civilized way by the supplier, then debt collection could be the only solution and the cause would be the intransigence of the debtor and not a management failure.

But debt collection only works if the debtor can pay.

In an age of corporate cowardice and buck-passing it is tempting to find excuses for debt collection and bad debts. Saying, 'we *couldn't have possibly known they were going broke,*' is futile if your business fails as a result. Some spectacular failures that have caused their suppliers' demise include Enron, Long Terms Capital Management (founded by Nobel Prize Winners) plus countless smaller businesses. To get a feel for the pain, in the margin write the names of businesses you know that have failed and dragged others down with them.

Just because so many outfits have collapsed and bankrupted their suppliers does not always mean that the suppliers are victims of circumstances beyond their control. Certainly, they did not have control over the fate of their debtor. But they did have control over the amount of credit they gave and when to stop it and get tough. In these cases, the bad debt incurred is caused by the creditor's management failing to recognize the escalating risk and not fixing it.

90% of the time, lengthening payment delay is the first sign of impending collapse. This is easy to spot because the account has simply not been paid. For outfits listed on the stock exchange, other danger signs include media reports of problems, losses, credit downgrades and drop, or collapse, of share price. Because of darn right lies by some chief executives and their collaborators, beware of claims that all is rosy, or soon will be. Non-listed and small businesses do not usually get media attention because they rarely broadcast the fact they are in trouble, so the media have few ways of finding out even if they were interested. But the fact that payment delays are worsening is a sign of problems, so unless fraud or deception is involved or out-of-the-blue catastrophes cause the collapse, the creditor's management is likely to be responsible for the bad debt.

Previous chapters help avoid the inconvenience of debt collection and bad debts, but like belting-up in a car or plane it is good to be prepared. Businesses in any sector can fail, but some industries are more prone to it than others, such as construction and hospitality. Take a few minutes to view the Dun & Bradstreet website and their payment analyses which sometimes highlight risky sectors. It can be better to lose business instead of going out of business by losing money and losses can be reduced or prevented by monitoring, so turn the tap off before getting scalded by heat or criticism.

Ways to avoid the heat are:

1. **Monitor the media and trade rumours for sign of problems;**
2. **Get new customers to complete a credit account application form – ask existing ones to do so too if not previously done** (say you have a new system and need to update the records);
3. **Do credit Checks before opening accounts – and on existing customers owing a lot and in arrears;**
4. **Try and get personal guarantees or other protection on large accounts;**
5. **Use effective credit control;**
6. **Stop supply if the amount owing threatens your survival.**

THE RHUBARB

Browsing through debt collection options is about as enjoyable as eating raw rhubarb for breakfast. The debt collection menu comprises of law firms and debt collection companies who have the biggest market share, plus freelance staff or former staff of collection and legal firms, private investigators, former police officers and thugs. Although debt collecting is a last resort and usually spells the end of customer relations, it does not have to be ruthless. Unless there is a genuine dispute, the sooner action is taken the better the chances of getting paid and the choices are:

- **Lawyers – especially for big and contentious debts**
- **Debt collectors – small to medium debts unless they cap their fees for big ones**
- **Small claims courts, disputes and resolution services**
- **DIY**

Some collection costs can be recovered, but may not be if the debtor pays immediately upon being contacted by your lawyer or debt collector. If full recovery costs are included in your terms of trade they can probably be recovered even if the debtor promptly pays in an attempt to pre-empt it.

LAWYERS

If your local lawyer has a collections unit, ask what the charges are and if they seem high, approach another lawyer.

A local lawyer or debt collector enables hearings to take place locally, which is handy if you have out of town or interstate debtors because to avoid losing the deter needs to defend themselves on your turf, or appoint someone to act on their behalf.

Lawyers and debt collectors have mixed performances as they cannot do the impossible, which is what those who have left it too late sometimes expect. Lawyers can be more expensive than debt collectors, but this may not be so for large sums as lawyers usually charge set fees based on time, whereas debt collectors' fees are usually a percentage of the debt. Debt collectors also need lawyers when push comes to shove and some have their own legal departments for court action and other things lawyers do.

DEBT COLLECTORS

When choosing a debt collector, select an ethical one that uses legal methods to obtain payment. Some of these are listed corporations, which indicate that debt collection is a profitable business to be in. Unethical debt collectors include gangs and other thugs who use threats, violence or illegal seizure of property to get debtors to pay. Such types have no role to play in lawful debt collection.

Debt collectors can be cheaper than lawyers because some only charge a fee if they succeed. But there are conditions, so find out what these are. As with lawyers, the costs might be recoverable from the debtor.

Some collectors are good at tracing those who have done-a-runner (they can be better at it than lawyers), but costs quickly escalate, especially if the debtor has gone interstate or overseas. When choosing a debt collector look at both national and local ones and as with lawyers, local ones can get debtors who are far away to promptly pay by stating they will start proceedings in your local court and not theirs. Some debt collectors can also act on your behalf in court provided the case is straightforward and the debt is not disputed.

An array of collectors pops up in web searches when entering *debt collectors* and a look at the fees section of their websites should tell you their charges and conditions, but some only reveal these by contacting them.

As in most sectors, some collectors (and lawyers) are better than others, so ask around if possible and avoid the rent-a-thug types.

SMALL CLAIMS COURT, DISPUTES AND RESOLUTION SERVICES

Where you live dictates what court or other options exist and in the US can vary from state to state. Australia, Canada and UK have small claims courts, (in Australia and Canada the maximum sums these courts will handle can vary in each state or province) and New Zealand and Australia also have disputes tribunals where the presence of lawyers can be detrimental to success! There is a cap on the amount the small claims courts and disputes tribunals will accept which are subject to change, so check them to see if your claim fits in because the costs are usually low.

Because lawyers and debt collectors are frowned upon in disputes tribunals, hearings are more informal and relaxed, but this does not mean they are sloppy or causal. Credit control and other staff are acceptable and insurance claim disputes are frequently heard.

DIY

Do-it-yourself debt collection is an option for businesses employing trained credit or accounts staff and can reduce collection costs. However, businesses in which DIY debt collection is possible are likely to have terms of trade that contain recovery cost clauses, so the economics of DIY debt collection could be dubious.

DIY could be profitable though if in-house recovery costs at commercial collection rates are stated in the terms of trade, so include them if they are not. If you have the staff, or the time, attending a seminar on debt collection can help you do some of it yourself, or perhaps all of it, which should be very little if the business is well run.

If yours is a small business, DIY debt collection is possible simply by sending the *dunning letter* in the *When to send final demands* chapter. That might be all that is needed to get paid. If so, you will get your money plus avoid recovery costs and stress.

Action Plan – plan now to be prepared.

<u>**My debt collection options are:**</u>

1. Lawyers (which) _____

_____

2. Debt collectors (which) _____

3. Small Claims Court or Disputes Tribunal (nearest one to me
is) _____

_____

4. DIY If needed, I will attend a debt collecting seminar Yes ☐
No ☐ If No, reason is _____

_____

5. Other options (if any) _____

_____

_____

_____

_____

LEGAL STUFF

Knowing whom, or what, you are dealing with might be a good idea when selling on credit.

Most English speaking countries have similar business structures, such as USA, Australia, Canada, UK, New Zealand, South Africa and much of the Commonwealth. If you live in one and sell to businesses in another on open account, for example USA to Canada and Australia to New Zealand, read the *Foreign trade* chapter.

But before going further, the author and publisher must state that the information in this chapter (and the entire book) outlines the basic types of businesses you are likely to sell on credit to and does not purport to be legal text or advice and must not be regarded as such. The types of organisations most businesses are likely to sell on credit to are: partnerships; sole traders or sole proprietors; businesses 'trading as...'; limited liability companies; incorporated societies; clubs; trusts and the dead.

With regard to the dead, they may not have been dead when they bought from you, but might be when the bill is due, so this is looked at too.

Different words are used to describe businesses in various countries, which are handy to know if buying or selling overseas. Common ones are *Limited* (Ltd), *Incorporated* (Inc) and both basically mean that you can't sue the shareholders if bills are not paid. When *Public Limited Company* (PLC) appears after the name it means it is listed on the stock exchange and again the shareholders cannot be sued. The shareholders of *Private Limited Companies* (*Limited* means limited liability) cannot normally be sued either and in some countries the abbreviations *Pty, Pvt, Pvte* are used to identify private companies. Some countries, such as New Zealand, don't bother to distinguish between them and just use *Limited* on the basis that it does not matter if they are public or private because both can escape their obligations if they go broke.

PARTNERSHIPS

Traditionally, a partnership was simply two or more people in business together and sometimes there was not even a written agreement. It is potentially risky to be a partner as each partner can be jointly and severally liable for the partnership's debts and other liabilities. You could sue any or all of the partners and if one cannot pay, the others have to, which means that a partner with only a 5% interest could have 100% liability.

Business partnership law in some countries, such as Australia and New Zealand, has barely changed for over a century. But potentially damaging changes from a payment aspect have occurred in most English speaking countries, which just might have originated from legal and accounting firms wanting to protect their own partners.

Not all partnership liabilities can be sidestepped but some can and more loopholes are likely to appear, so if you sell to partnerships ask the partners if they can or have wriggled out of personal liability. If they say 'no' and it turns out they have fibbed, you have been deceived and they could be personally liable if you suffer a loss. If you think they are fibbing, contact your lawyer or get personal guarantees or other securities.

SOLE TRADERS

Ronnie McDonald is a sole trader and the sole proprietor of his business and does not trade as a limited liability company or a limited partnership. As a result, Ronnie is personally liable for his business and personal debts. If sole traders or sole proprietors cannot pay they can be personally sued or bankrupted. It is as simple as that, or is at time of writing, but that might change too.

'TRADING AS...'

If Ronnie McDonald's septic tank emptying service trades as McDonald's Takeaways (this business existed until somebody asked them to kindly change the name and the truck's name was Big Mac, as was the license plate) he is still personally liable for the debts of McDonald's Takeaways. If Ronnie claims he is not liable, he is mistaken.

If a sole trader, or someone 'trading as...', gets smart and forms a limited liability company, such as McDonalds Takeaways Ltd/Inc he could claim to be a 'corporate' and try to avoid paying previous bills. But if Ronnie forgets to tell you about his new corporate status, you would believe he was still a sole trader. If he owes heaps he could say, *'I am now a limited liability company and you can't bankrupt me, so there!'* If he had deliberately avoided telling you this to avoid personal liability, call his bluff and sue him personally. If it is shown that he formed the company to avoid paying his creditors who were supplying him, and not his new company, in good faith you could sue or bankrupt him, especially for debts incurred before the formation and possibly for those incurred afterwards.

However, Ronnie is now a smart alec and says, *'I wrote to you telling you of this,'* or *'I phoned you/your accounts department and you said it was OK'* or *'For months I have been ordering from you and paying you from Ronnie McDonald Takeaways Pty Limited, so you have known for ages that you are now dealing with a company.'*

This is a grey area, and can boil down to credibility. If he has really been ordering and paying from Ronnie McDonald Takeaways Pty Ltd for some time, then regrettably you should have known about the change as there have been judgements supporting this. So, if you have supplied goods he has ordered in the name of his company, then it probably means you have accepted the orders in the company name, even if you have continued to invoice them in his personal name.

Check to see who is ordering from you and paying you. Is it still good old Ronnie, or is it now Ronnie McDonald Takeaways Pty Ltd?

LIMITED LIABILITY COMPANIES

The shareholders of a limited liability company cannot normally be sued. It is possible to sue the directors personally in some circumstances, but in practice this can be hard. This is why limited liability companies are so popular.

However, before giving up and writing off a debt from a limited liability company if they refuse to pay or cannot pay, try this:

Did they order the goods from you knowing they could not pay for them? If so, the directors may be guilty of trading while insolvent or of reckless trading and could be personally liable.

Do you have a personal guarantee from a director or shareholder? If so, they could be personally liable or at least have a strong incentive to ensure that the company pays.

Check to see if they really are a limited company. They may be kidding you and if so the person placing the orders could be personally liable.

Can you repossess your goods? An administrator, receiver, liquidator will automatically say no, but call their bluff if bankruptcy or other protective laws do not apply.

Can you become a priority creditor by withholding further supplies or retaining artwork or other property? If these are crucial, dig in and demand full payment.

Is the share capital fully paid up? If not, there may be some money available especially if no receiver has been appointed and you issue a winding-up order.

If they owe you a lot, don't simply quit. It may only take a short while to get paid, even if it is just to get you off their back.

INCORPORATED SOCIETIES

These are in many ways similar to limited liability companies, so treat them the same if your exposure is not high. If it is high, ask them to explain their legal structure and who is responsible for payment if they default or get them to pay cash if they are not regular customers.

UNINCORPORATED SOCIETIES OR CLUBS

You could sue the individual who placed the order as unincorporated clubs are not legal entities. This is something to be aware of if you belong to an unincorporated club and you order goods or supplies – perhaps the venue hire, drinks or food for the next exhibition. If purchases are infrequent get them to pay by credit card or cash.

TRUSTS

The main reason business people form trusts is to protect their personal assets and to avoid paying you if their business collapses. A lawyer once said to me, *'If I was a director I would have no personal assets in my name!'*

Trust laws vary and you may not know that your customers' assets are protected by a trust as either you haven't the time to find out or cannot find out. From an asset protection aspect there are two basic types of trusts: the family trust or a trust that carries out a business or activity, such as a property trust or an incorporated charity trust. In a trust that is involved in a business or similar undertaking the trustees can be personally liable for debts, but you must check this. They may have contracted out of the liability by stating, possibly in small print, that you are selling to the trust without liability on them. Also, their personal assets may be protected by another trust, or even a river of trusts, that could cost a fortune and a lot of time to unravel.

THE DEAD

The definition of dead is about the same in most countries and whilst they were alive when they placed the order they might not be when it is time to pay. If they were already dead when they placed the order then unless it was their ghost that placed it, somebody has committed a fraud.

Problems with deceased customers are more likely to arise with sole traders, sole practitioners or sole directors and shareholders of small companies. Taxes and debts follow people to the grave, or at least to their estate, but it might take time for payment to be made and proof of debt forms may be required, which can be straightforward but time consuming so your lawyer may be needed. Bigger outfits find replacements for the deceased, but expect delays if the deceased was the finance director, treasurer or other person who pays the accounts.

VOIDABLE PREFERENCE

Voidable preference is a real threat if you succeed in getting paid but the customer later goes broke. This nasty little law penalises the diligent and business-like by legally stealing money that was paid to them up to six months ago and giving it to the less diligent or undeserving. If you have been paid by a business that goes broke after paying you, expect to be contacted by a receiver or liquidator demanding repayment. You will probably know that the business has gone out of business and if so you have advance warning, so speak to your lawyer, preferably before the demand letter or call comes. If it arrives before getting legal advice, refuse to discuss it. If they threaten you, call your lawyer right away - see *Risk* chapter.

Action Plan – do it now if you have high exposure.

I sell on credit to:

Partnerships	Yes☐	Is my exposure large?	Yes☐
Sole traders or sole proprietors	Yes☐	Is my exposure large?	Yes☐
Businesses 'trading as...'	Yes☐	Is my exposure large?	Yes☐
Limited liability companies	Yes☐	Is my exposure large?	Yes☐
Incorporated societies	Yes☐	Is my exposure large?	Yes☐
Unincorporated societies or clubs	Yes☐	Is my exposure large?	Yes☐
Trusts	Yes☐	Is my exposure large?	Yes☐
Someone now dead or dying	Yes☐	Is my exposure large?	Yes☐
Other (if any)	Yes☐	Is my exposure large?	Yes☐

For those ticked Yes and where exposure is large, I will:

Seek legal advice from _____ (name)

Do the following _____

_____

_____

_____

_____

TERMS & CONDITIONS
OF TRADE

Sound Terms & conditions of trade can prevent disaster when nasty things happen.

Terms of trade help shield you from events that are not your fault, such as the purchaser failing to comply with your products' safety instructions or misuse of the product, disputes and what your remedies are if they don't pay. They also define delivery, warranty, product return policy, interest on unpaid accounts if they pay late, recovery of debt collection costs and other conditions applicable to your business.

If you do not have terms of trade, seriously think about getting them as soon as possible because at some stage you are almost certain to encounter a problem and terms of trade could resolve it without drama. The following is a partial example:

GOOD SERVICE COMPANY
TERMS AND CONDITIONS OF TRADE

PRICING
We reserve the right to alter our prices by giving one month's...

ORDERING
Orders must be made on a valid purchase order...

DELIVERY
Delivery shall be defined as...

RISK/INSURANCE
Risk in the goods passes to you as purchaser as soon as ...

WARRANTIES
All warranties expire upon payment of invoice unless...

RETURNS
No return of goods will be accepted unless...

PAYMENT TERMS PAYMENTS
All products must be paid for in cash unless ...
rates...

INTEREST ON OVERDUE

Interest at 2% more than standard credit card interest

LIABILITY
The maximum amount for which we can have liability is ...

RETENTION OF TITLE
Title in the products shall remain with the company until...

COLLECTION COSTS
The full costs of recovery including legal fees and...

LIEN
We have a possessory lien on goods...

SECURITY FOR PAYMENT
If we allow you additional time to pay any indebtedness ...

SET OFF
We shall be entitled to set off against any monies owed ...

Keep your terms of trade to the point and avoid legalese or jargon. If you sell cups and saucers, you are unlikely to need terms of trade 10 pages long, but they do need to specify what your liabilities are if the handles break and the bottoms fall out.

Ideally, the terms should be one page or less so they can be printed on the back of invoices. This helps remind slow payers of their obligations during credit control, especially interest charges, debt collection costs, retention of title, repossession and not releasing goods or work in progress. If their account is in arrear and other credit control methods have failed, saying something like the following can fix it;

'If we receive payment tomorrow (or in three days but no more than a week) **we will not charge you 20% interest as shown on the terms of trade on the back of our invoice and on the terms of trade you signed. We don't want to do this and by paying now you will avoid it. Will you pay today?'**

If you already have effective terms of trade, insert the above or similar wording in *Action Plan* at the end of the *Telephone credit control* chapter to make credit control more effective. If you do not have terms of trade or they are unsatisfactory, insert it when they are complete.

Most businesses should have terms of trade, but it could be downright silly for a very small business, such as an owner-operated house window cleaner, lawn mowing service, newsstand or a small café to have terms of trade, so take a sensible commercial view. If there is a risk a window could break because of (say) its position, point this out to the customer and say that if you attempt to clean it you will not accept liability if it breaks.

If you are a small business or just starting-up and cannot afford a lawyer, look at the terms of trade of established businesses in comparable sectors as yours to see what they include. Do not use them without permission because they will be copyright and you could be in trouble if you pirate them. But if you have suppliers in a comparable industry and if their terms of trade could apply to your business ask for permission to use them, or a modification thereto. Because you are their customer they should at least consider it as it will not cost them anything. If they are mean and refuse, ask them why and say you will take your business to any of their rivals who agree to it!

When you can afford it, approach a commerce lawyer and ask how much they will charge to compile terms and conditions of trade. Family lawyers can be inexperienced in commercial law, so select commerce specialists and approach three to compare costs.

If your terms of trade contain the commonly used retention of title clause (commonly called the *Romalpa Clause*) it could be unenforceable. Changes to retention of title (ownership) have occurred in some countries which now make the earlier tried-and-tested retention of title clauses obsolete. These are often called a *Romalpa clause* after a UK court case involving Romalpa Aluminium which ruled that ownership of goods only passed to the purchaser upon payment in full of all monies outstanding, including unpaid money for other purchases. This meant that the seller retained ownership until the buyer had paid everything. It was so successful that many countries adopted Romalpa-type clauses.

But unknown to you, the debtor's bank, or almost anybody else, could now own your goods regardless of what your terms of trade state. The debtor could even register them as his personal property (or that of his mother or anyone else) as security for loans or other favours. This prevents you from repossessing what you thought was your property and you might not be able to retain work in progress either because it too could be owned by a bank, or anybody but you. Your accountant or lawyer should be aware of such changes, so ask them to keep you informed.

Key *getting paid* points in your terms of trade include:

1. **Ownership** – title must remain with you until all outstanding money is paid and not just the money for one sale. Beware of law changes that could affect title.
2. **Withholding property** – retain possession of work in progress and other materials as a lever for getting paid.
3. **Recovery costs** – claim **the full** debt collection costs which includes legal and court costs, debt collection charges, out-of-pocket expenses such as time and travel and all other applicable costs.
4. **Interest** – interest rates in old-fashioned terms of trade are often so low they are an invitation to become your customer's bank. To be a deterrent, charge 2% to 5% more than the Visa, MasterCard or Amex standard interest rates. State that it is effective from the date of sale, or when payment was due, otherwise you might not be able to make it retrospective. Offer to waive it if they promptly pay - if they still don't, it could be because they cannot pay, so then act quickly...
5. **Personal guarantees** – for guarantees to be valid they need to be constructed by a capable lawyer. Whilst guarantees are often left out of terms of trade, it is useful to have a reference to them.

6. **Disputes** – include a dispute resolution clause enabling you to obtain payment for sales that are not disputed. Charge interest if they do not pay.

7. **Ordering** – specify what constitutes an order and ensure you comply with customers' ordering requirements because failing to do so is a reason for late payment.

There may be other clauses applicable to your business, so include them too.

Terms of trade accompany *Credit Application Forms* (see Chapter 7) and get prospective customers to sign both before giving credit.

ACTION PLAN

☐ My terms of trade are excellent.   Yes ☐ No ☐
   If Yes, diarise next review
☐ I will obtain terms of trade/review them by (date)_____
☐ I will approach this/these people to compile/review
   them
   1_____ (name)
   2_____ (name)
   3_____ (name)
☐ Other actions (if needed) _____
   _____
   _____
   _____
   _____
   _____

FOREIGN TRADE

If trading with other countries, knowing the difference in expressions helps prevent making a takeover bid when all you want is to buy or sell goods.

In America, *stock* means shareholding, while in Australia, UK, New Zealand and elsewhere, *stock* means inventory. If a customer in those countries says they want to buy stock, it means they want to buy goods and are not making a takeover offer.

It can be unbusinesslike (meaning you might lose the sale) if you don't grant normal credit facilities for sales to neighbours, such as Australia to New Zealand and USA to Canada and vice versa, or UK to some EC countries. But if payment issues arise there might be problems in getting judgements or getting your goods back caused by differences in laws, commercial custom and distance. So, before sending stuff over the sea or border on open account, get the customer to complete your normal Credit Application Form and to sign your Terms and Conditions of Sale, (add a clause saying the sale is governed by your laws and not theirs) which can be sent and returned by fax or email in the same way as domestic sales. Then do credit checks as you would at home. In the English-speaking world they can be just as easy to do as they are at home, apart from the cost of calls, which with Skype or similar are effectively free. If you do not use Skype or have cheap overseas rates, buy a phone card.

But where possible, avoid selling on credit to overseas customers because it is not just payment and repossession that can cause problems, retention of title can too as covered in the *Terms & Conditions of Trade* chapter. Although Australia, Canada, New Zealand UK and USA have similar payment records (some pay a bit later than others but not by much), other trading partners, such as the Pacific Islands for Australia and New Zealand, Mexico and the Caribbean for USA and Canada and Spain, Italy and Greece for UK have different ideas on paying accounts. To save problems, obtain prepayment for sales to island states because *island time* also applies to payment time.

Currency fluctuations are a possible issue for open account sales to other countries and it is safer to invoice customers in your currency and not theirs, unless you like the thrill of foreign exchange gains (or losses). Invoicing and obtaining payment in your currency also applies to other overseas sales whatever the payment method is, but the US Dollar is the main currency for international trade but you can hedge against losses through your bank. If you sell internationally on the internet, speak to your bank or accountant about currency hedging and exchange rate risks and opportunities.

Consignment stock can be a problem regardless of whether you are selling on consignment within the country or outside it. *Consignment* means that the buyer only pays when the goods are sold, which can apply to the wine trade and other sectors. The problem with consignment stock is auditing because unless the customer is close by, you either have to take their word that the goods remain unsold or get someone to check. Consignment stock can be on a *sale-or-return* basis, which means that if it is not sold you have to take it back and unless you have made payment of return freight a condition of sale, you will probably have to pay the freight as an incentive for them to return it. Try and avoid consignment stock even for domestic sales and for overseas sales the cost of return freight can be high.

It is risky selling on credit to businesses in countries with a poor payment record or those short of foreign exchange, especially if they are combined with import and exchange control regulations. This means virtually all of Africa, much of Latin America, some Pacific islands, The Middle East, parts of Asia and parts of Europe. It is also costly trying to recover overseas debt and can be impossible. The safest way of selling overseas is by irrevocable and confirmed letters of credit drawn on a first class bank. Giving credit to individuals living overseas should also be avoided. If they cannot pay by credit card or direct credit before dispatch, think twice before sending your goods.

If you are exporting, or would like to, arrange payment before dispatch and the following are the standard ones:

• **Documents on Acceptance** (D/A). The original shipping documents and invoices are sent to your bank, which send them to a bank in the importer's country along with a bill of exchange or draft. When the importer signs the draft the bank releases the documents and the importer clears the goods through customs and takes possession. The draft or bill can be payable on sight (immediate payment) or for a term of 30 to 90 days (or longer) depending on what you have agreed with the importer. Obtaining immediate payment, less commission and interest, for term drafts is possible provided the importer's credit rating is high. D/A is not totally risk free because it is possible that the bill will not be honoured and by then the importer may possess your goods and you might never get them back.

- **Letter of Credit (L/C)**. This is the safest method of payment and L/Cs are formal payment instruments used internationally. Because they are effectively risk free, L/Cs are preferred because the only risk is if the bank fails (hmm). The documentation and terms used in L/Cs are very precise and care is needed, but your bank can assist (they make lots of money out of trade finance). There are two main types of L/C – *revocable* and *irrevocable* – both of which come in two versions (**confirmed** and **not confirmed/unconfirmed**). The safest one to use is a **confirmed irrevocable letter of credit** which is not supposed to bounce unless both your bank and the buyer's bank go bust. The other documentation requirements are similar to those for D/A. This may all seem confusing, but it is really quite straightforward when you have done it once or twice.

- **Bank bill**. These are bills of exchange that a bank issues or endorses, which means they will not bounce as long as the bank doesn't fold. They can be issued at sight (which means payment on presentation of the bill), or at a fixed date and for term bills 30 to 90 days is common. Term bills can be discounted and if your bank does this, you can get the money immediately, less the discount. Speak to your bank if you wish to know more about bank bills and drafts.

- **Bank drafts, direct credit and internet banking**. A bank draft is a bank cheque (which is not supposed to bounce) that is mailed to you. Your bank is likely to charge a modest commission when you deposit it. It is cheaper and quicker for customers to pay by direct credit or funds transfer by internet banking if the customer's bank or country allows it

- **Credit cards**. These are usually only suitable for modest amounts and it depends on the buyer's credit card limit and the card company's commission.

For D/A and L/Cs documentation requirements have to be carefully followed to avoid payment delays. They include invoices (4 copies or more), insurance, which is usually cost, insurance and freight (CIF) plus sometimes 10%. Marine insurance has options for general and specific average. This is because the shipper shares the voyage risk with the ship owner, which is a custom going back to Phoenician traders several thousand years ago. If the ship is damaged or sinks the shipping company levies a charge (average) up to the value of the cargo and is payable by each cargo owner, or shipper. Banks are unlikely to issue irrevocable letters of credit without insurance and a bill of lading from a shipping company or air waybill is needed as proof of dispatch. These come with originals (there can be more than one original) and copies of the original. Original bills of lading and air waybills are proof of ownership and the cargo will not be released until they are surrendered. These and all other documentation are sent by your bank to their correspondence bank who releases them to the buyer upon the buyer's acceptance of the letter of credit.

ACTION PLAN

This is how foreign customers will pay.

Will I give credit to foreign customers? Yes ☐ No ☐ and the reasons are _____

_____

_____

I will ensure my retention of title clause is valid in my customer's country   Yes ☐

I will grant normal credit facilities to these customers:

Name	Reasons
1.	
2.	
3.	

I will not grant credit to these/this type of customer:

Name	Reasons
1.	
2.	
3.	

LET'S GO A-COURTING

Disclaimer. This is a guide only and it is not legal advice and must not be regarded as such.

So, despite your best efforts you still haven't got your money? What to do next depends on:

- How much they owe.
- Is there a dispute.
- Do you have the debtor's full contact details.
- Do you have terms of trade that allow you to recover full collection costs.
- Can the debtor pay and are they likely to go broke.

There is a rule-of-thumb method of calculating whether a debt is worth chasing called the *Economic Collection Formula*. To apply it you need to estimate the odds of getting paid versus the collection costs you will incur.

The accuracy of the Economic Collection Formula depends upon the user's ability to calculate the likelihood of success (Confidence of Recovery). People tend to be overly optimistic and overestimate their chances of success, so be realistic and avoid gritting your teeth and convincing yourself that you are going to recover the debt if the facts indicate otherwise. Although you may feel determined to recover the debt, remain objective. So, take a deep breath and calmly ask yourself, 'How likely am I to recover the debt?

To determine the Chance of Recovery, use the following formula and the bullet points at the beginning of this chapter.

Economic Collection Formula					
Confidence of Recovery	Chance of Recovery	Amount Owing	Likely amount Recovered*	Collection Costs	Decision
Very confident	90-95%	$2,000	$1,800	$400	attempt to recover
Sort of confident	80%	$2,000	$1,600	$400	attempt to recover
A bit of doubt	70%	$2,000	$1,400	$400	attempt to recover
Could be 50/50	50%	$2,000	$1,000	$400	attempt to recover
Doubtful	25%	$2,000	$ 500	$400	very borderline
Very doubtful	10%	$2,000	$ 200	$400	not worth it

* The likely amount recovered is what, on average, you would receive for every $2,000 owing to you multiplied by the recovery % in the second column.

IF THE DEBTOR HAS 'DONE A RUNNER'

If the debtor has disappeared, then the chances of recovery are very limited as they have to be found and their identity proven. If they have gone, or live, overseas, the chances of success are very low and collection costs very high. Also, you may be liable for collection costs regardless of whether the debtor is traced or not. Because of this, if you are selling on credit across borders, be very thorough with credit checks and if a patchy payment record is revealed, get them to pay in advance, or by letter of credit, bank bill, bank draft or documents on acceptance as outlined in the *Foreign trade* chapter.

If the debtor is a company and the directors have disappeared, then you have to find them – probably incurring more costs than for finding an individual, then proving they have a personal liability to pay. This may be hard to impossible and costly.

Some debt collectors have overseas branches or alliances that may be able to help, providing you know which country your debtor has fled to. If you do not know where they are, be prepared for big bills and little success. If you know where they are, be prepared for big bills and then estimate the chances of success using the Economic Collections formula. Then get a quotation of the debt collection fees and insert these into the formula. It might be hard to get a quotation, but you should get a reasonable estimate and beware of the possibility of costs escalating.

BANKRUPTCY

If the debtor is an individual or a sole trader who has been declared bankrupt, then in reality you probably have to write the debt off. If they are not bankrupt, then you may be able to bankrupt them unless they pay you. If the debtor is a partnership and some of the partners are not bankrupt you can sue them.

RECEIVERSHIPS AND LIQUIDATION

If the debtor is a company and is in receivership or liquidation, then your claim needs to be lodged with the receiver or liquidator. As an unsecured creditor, which is what you are likely to be, you will be very lucky to get paid in full and also lucky if you receive a percentage of the debt, which more often than not is only a small one. If it is in administration, you might be asked to settle for a proportion of the debt and administrators can be obligated to treat all unsecured creditors the same and not show favour to just some of them. Receivers and others have been known to make exceptional payments to an unsecured creditor if they are crucial to the 'going concern' value of the business. However, you must be a crucial supplier to the business and the receiver or administrator has to assess whether it is a going concern.

Receivers and others have been known to bully crucial suppliers into continuing to sell goods on credit without being paid for goods purchased prior to receivership. Be extremely firm with them and ignore any threats such as, *'We will inform the media that as a result of you withholding supply, hundreds of jobs will be lost.'* It was not you who put them into receivership. It was the debenture holder, perhaps a bank, who, with the receiver, is responsible. You are a victim of their actions too.

In many receiverships there is little possibility of the business remaining a going concern, and little hope of unsecured creditors receiving anything.

Liquidations are similar, but can be lengthy. We know one that started in 1985 and it was only finalised in 2004 – 19 years later. It was a UK/USA investment company in which the founder embezzled nearly all the investors' funds, including some of the author's. There was a sort-of happy ending as 20% was recovered from the sale of a French chateaux the founder had bought . Although the embezzler went to jail in USA, he is now free, but still refuses to cooperate with the authorities over where the rest of the money went. Whilst this affair is small change in comparison to Bernard Madoff's billions of dollars fraud and conviction in 2009, it illustrates how long it can take to get even a modest payment.

Most liquidations are more straightforward as there are usually no assets to find, and little chance of any payment to creditors.

DEBT COLLECTORS

If you already have a debt collector, and they are good to average, then use them. Do not hesitate – you may not know how close the debtor is to going bust.

Debt collection fees vary. Some offer a no success/no fee option, but ask them about this as conditions and fishhooks may apply. Others charge a minimum fee and a sliding scale ranging from 5 to 20% depending on the amount of the debt. In addition to their fees, extra costs are levied for court action and the services of recovery or field agents or other outside parties. Total collection costs can be significant and can be greater than the debt. While reputable collectors should tell you the total amount of all fees, check them carefully. Use the *Economic Collections Formula* before committing yourself. Even if your terms of trade allow you to recover all collection costs, you may still be liable for the collector's disbursements or other charges if recovery action fails.

LAWYERS

Lawyers charge a fee whether the debt is recovered or not and it can be a coin-toss deciding whether to use a lawyer or a debt collector. Either way, don't delay the decision ...

SMALL CLAIMS COURTS

The amounts Small Claims Courts can handle varies in each jurisdiction. If the debt is a bit more than the maximum amount it may be worth reducing it to get it before the court as costs are low.

You need to be certain your case is strong, otherwise you could lose. Look objectively at your claim through the debtor's eyes and if there is a plausible dispute the court may dismiss your claim entirely, or only award part of it. Lawyers may be allowed at Small Claims hearings but it can pay not to have one as you might get a more sympathetic hearing - it's also cheaper of course. Small Claims Courts are often less formal than Magistrates' Courts and cases can be decided more on merit rather than on the finer points of law, but don't bank on it.

The magistrate or arbitrator can act as a referee and if you win, a judgement is made in your favour and this can affect the debtor's credit record. At anytime during the hearing either party can propose a settlement (say 50%) and, if accepted by the other party, that's the end of it. This can enable the debtor to avoid a judgement being made against them to protect their credit record. It also enables you to compromise if your case is not as strong as you thought it was.

You, or a member of your staff, will have to attend the hearing as a no-show means you lose. If you attend but the debtor does not and has not asked for a deferment, you normally win. Whilst it is not always as clear cut as that, courts often take a dim view of those who fail to attend. The debtor though might later argue that the documents were not served, so ensure they are personally delivered or at least sent by registered post.

Unfortunately, getting a judgement in your favour and then getting paid can be another story. If you win, then whilst still in court try and ask the debtor how they will pay. *'Can you give me a cheque right now?'* or, if you accept credit cards, have a voucher and fill in their credit card details there and then, or in the corridor. Try and get a promise to pay immediately. Waive the judgement at them and follow them to their office if necessary whilst they are still reeling at the shock of losing and their defences are in disarray.

DISPUTES TRIBUNAL

Some countries, such as Australia, have now adopted the Disputes Tribunal concept that originated in New Zealand and other countries are looking at it. As the name implies, Disputes Tribunals are for dispute resolution, so use the tribunal if your debtor disputes the debt and the amount is within the limit - at time of writing $7,500, or up to $12,000 if both parties agree to a hearing. However, the Tribunal can only accept the case if the debtor disputes the debt and your case needs to be strong, otherwise you could lose. Look objectively at the debtor's dispute. If it is a genuine dispute, the tribunal may dismiss your claim entirely, or only award part of it. If your case is strong but the amount is above the limit, it might be it may be worth reducing it to get it before the tribunal.

The cost of lodging claims is modest and no lawyers are allowed at Disputes Tribunal hearings. The case is decided on its merits and both parties attend and the decision is made by a tribunal referee. If you win, a judgement is made in your favour and this can affect the debtor's credit record. At anytime during the hearing either party can propose a settlement, and if accepted by the other party, that's the end of it. A negotiated settlement can enable the debtor to avoid a judgement being made against them to protect their credit record, as well as enabling you to compromise if your case starts to look flimsy.

As the debtor will only bring their evidence to the tribunal on the day of the hearing, you may not have advance warning of what it will be. To avoid surprises, it is a good idea to be sure of your facts. You, or a member of your staff, will have to attend the hearing and a no-show means you lose. If the debtor does not show-up, then you win. While it is not always as clear-cut as that, Tribunal referees often take a very dim view of those who fail to attend.

Unfortunately, getting a judgement in your favour and then getting paid can be another story. Disputes Tribunal referees can sometimes be a bit more lenient with their time than judges or magistrates and allow you to arrange payment options in the hearing room while they are still present. If you win, then in front of the referee ask the debtor how they are going to pay as described in the last paragraph in the *Small Claims Court* section.

GUARANTEES AND SECURITIES

If you have a personal guarantee from the debtor, now is the time to use it. Sometimes just hinting that you are going to is all that is needed to get them to pay.

Personal guarantees can be hard to enforce unless they have been constructed by a good lawyer and precisely executed. Guarantees have been set aside on such grounds as being signed by the debtor under duress, for instance, '*I needed the goods in an emergency, so I signed the form without reading it or being fully informed as to what I was signing.*'

However, a properly executed guarantee should stand these tests, provided the guarantor can pay that is. Even a more flimsy guarantee may hold up in court, especially in the Small Claims Court or Disputes Tribunal, but don't bank on it.

If you have retention of title in your terms of trade, such as the commonly called Romalpa clause, and if law changes have not made them obsolete and your goods have serial numbers or other identification that can accurately set them apart from other goods, then you may be able to repossess them.

LITIGATION

Going a-courting is costly, so look at the Economic Collections formula and the following box before calling your lawyer.

1. How much do they owe? Is it worth suing them?	Yes ☐ No ☐
2. Can they pay you if you win?	Yes ☐ No ☐
3. Do you know the debtor's full address for serving documents?	Yes ☐ No ☐
4. Could they have a good defence?	Yes ☐ No ☐
5. If they lose, will it harm them a lot?	Yes ☐ No ☐

Score: If you answer *No* to 1, 2 and 3 and *Yes* to 4, hesitate before suing. If you answer *Yes* to 1, 2, 3 and 5 and *No* to 4 then sue them.

It can be unprofitable and not much fun going to court. Even if you win, you still might not get paid if the debtor has gone into receivership or bankruptcy. The odds are they will have already gone broke if the reason they have not paid is because they have no money. Prevention is better than cure and good credit control helps prevent complex, and costly, problems arising.

HAVE FUN BY BANKRUPTING OR LIQUIDATING POOR PAYERS

Yes, it's true! You can have fun by bankrupting or liquidating those who have not paid, if you regard doing so as fun and have the time and money. It works like this:

First take out your cheque book and be prepared to spend $2,000 to $3,000 when you go and see your lawyer. But refer to the *Economic Collections Formula* to see if it is worth it. In the *Collection Costs* column of the formula insert $2,000-$3,000 and in the *Amount Owing* column insert the value of the debt to see what the chances of getting paid are if you start bankruptcy action against them (or threaten to). In the case of bankrupting an individual, to further assess the likelihood of getting paid, ask yourself if they will pay to avoid being declared bankrupt. If they really cannot pay, then what is the point of spending upwards of $2,000 to bankrupt them and not receiving anything for it?

If they are a company, the threat of winding up may persuade them to pay – that is, if they can pay. This seems to work as lots of winding up actions do not proceed to liquidations, so the assumption is they pay to avoid liquidation.

DIY

Of course it is possible to do much of the above yourself if you are experienced, but the real issue in that case is should you? Look at the value of your time and the costs to your business by diverting resources to DIY credit control, debtor management and debt collecting.

If you are self-employed, or a small business with few staff, getting tomorrows business today instead of chasing yesterday's money tomorrow may be more profitable. If so, outsourcing your credit control, or your total debtor administration may be cheaper and more effective as discussed in the *Outsourcing, factoring and other options* chapter.

ACTION PLAN

Who should really be looking after my debtors? Me ☐ My staff ☐ Why ___

_____

_____

Should I Outsource it?   Yes ☐ No ☐
Why _____

_____

How often should I review the above?
  Quarterly
  Half yearly
  Annually
Then diarise your answer so you do it)
Other options are _____

_____

_____

_____

31

TIMING

Timing is essential. Getting tough too soon with your debtors risks losing their custom. Getting tough too late risks losing your money.

There are few hard and fast rules and the timing for getting tough depends on the circumstances. As shown in the *Get paid NOW* and *Risk* chapters the longer a debt is left, the greater your risk.

Credit control rules-of-thumb for non-crippling debts are:

*   **If you give end of following month terms** encourage your debtors to pay on due date by calling them mid month to find out if your invoices are in the payment system. If not, find out why and fix any problems. If they are in the system, ask if they will be paid on due date. Doing this **reduces** the time needed for credit control instead of increasing it. To make it more enjoyable, at the same time ask if they need to reorder. This makes the call a sales tool as well, so you get paid and get more business.

- **If they have not paid on due date**, contact them one day later because a quick call reminding them of their payment promise could bring the money in without further fuss.

- **If they still haven't paid in seven days, or have broken a payment promise,** contact them again. Be more assertive this time, but not threatening or abusive, as shown in the *Telephone credit control* chapter. You could email or fax them, but calls can be quicker and work better.

- **If they do not pay in the next a few days (or a week at most)**, phone them again or send an email or fax.

- **If they have not paid after two weeks (maximum three) of due date,** escalate the urgency of phone or fax contacts. Resend **Fax 1** with handwritten comments about their broken promises, or send **Fax 2**.

- **Phone or fax them again before month end** otherwise they will slip into the 30 day and over column. Try and prevent this because payment for other sales made to them will then be due and getting money for two month's sales is harder than getting the money for one month's.

- **If they slip into the 30 day and over column, suspend their account** – do this if they owe heaps and default could damage you, or seriously consider doing it if the amount is not threatening. Perhaps give three to five days notice before closing the account to increases the incentive to pay. If they have placed further orders, only supply small ones and withhold large orders to prevent them buying up big before the account is closed.

* **If they do not pay at 45 days** definitely close their account and begin the recovery tactics shown in this book.

* **60 days and over.** If they have still not paid by now and there are no other issues, the only reason for non-payment is lack of money. There is now a problem and a bad debt risk, so look at the options you have written in the Action Plan boxes.

* **90 days.** Read chapter 2 again and take recovery action if not already underway.

The rule-of-thumb for credit control is: What will happen to me if they do not pay. If it could cripple or bankrupt me I will take immediate action and go to their premises if needed.

RECOVERY ACTION

Use this book as a guide to what the best options are. Decide which one to use, then act very quickly.

Getting paid is fun because you will have more money. That lowers your costs and increases your profits, which makes it even better.

Keep this book handy and use it *before* lack of cash caused by poor paying debtors threatens to swamp your business.

To stop that happening, never go easy on asking for your money and as Winston Churchill said, *'Never give in, never give in, never, never, never, never: in nothing great or small, large or petty – never give in – except to convictions of honour and good sense.'*

SUMMARY

This is what I will do to keep my debtors in good shape:

1. Complete all Action Plan boxes (if not done) Done ☐ Will do by _____(date)

2. My recovery options are:

Recover my property ☐

Withhold material in my possession ☐

Take formal recovery action ☐ using _____(names)

I will take action by _____(date)

Buy my debtors a copy of this book ☐

3. Other options are _____

_____

_____

_____

www.ingramcontent.com/pod-product-compliance
Lightning Source LLC
Chambersburg PA
CBHW051515170526
45165CB00002B/479